Is That the Best You Can Do?

A Tragedy-Born Guide to Living with No Regrets

Jim Philhower

A Tribute to Cole Philhower #49

CONTENTS

Part IV: Be a Servant Leader

Part V: Enjoy Life by Being Present

Part VI: Leave a Legacy

"I have loved the stars too fondly
to be fearful of the night."

Sarah Williams in "The Old Astronomer to His Pupil,"
as quoted by Cole Philhower

INTRODUCTION

1

CHAPTER ONE

The Phone Call

~~~~~~~~~~~~~~~~~~~~~~~~~~~~

I never get to scream that day.

Friday, June 27th, 2014. 9:00 a.m. I'm in my office at work. I'm on the phone booking a flight to Key West, Florida in August for me and my eighteen-year-old son and only child, Cole. He has just graduated high school. We love traveling together. This will be our last trip together before he heads off to college at Benedictine University in Chicago, where he will major in business and play NCAA lacrosse. We are planning on golfing, fishing, and having fun together in Key West.

I book the flight and hang up. Just as I reach to pick up the phone to book the hotel, it rings.

"This is Jim," I answer.

"It's me." It sounds like Cole in a very emotional voice.

"Hey bud, what's wrong?"

"No, it's me." It's Cole's mother, Jennifer. (We had divorced a few years ago.)

"What's wrong? Are you okay?"

"Cole's been in an accident. He is dead. The sheriff is at my house. You need to come here right now."

I'm instantly plunged into a state of shock. Brief pause. I ask Jennifer something. She cuts me off: "You need to get here now."

I stand up, shaking and in disbelief. "No, it can't be," I moan softly.

I burst through my office door and rush to the office of my boss, John. His door is closed. I throw the door open and see he's on the phone. He immediately knows something is wrong. "Hang up the phone," I hear myself say. He does.

"Jen just called. Cole's been in an accident. She said he's dead."

Without waiting for a response, I spin around and race out of John's office.

"What?" I hear him spluttering behind me. "Wait! You're not driving yourself."

I don't wait. I start jogging, my mind and heart racing. As I rush past my assistant I bark at her to cancel all my appointments for the day.

It's a twenty-five-minute drive from my office to Jen's house. I have no idea how many stop signs and red lights I speed through. My body is shaking and numb. I keep repeating out loud, "No, it can't be true. Cole's not dead. He's too big, too strong. It can't be."

I pull up to Jen's house and see two unmarked police vehicles. I storm into the house bursting with questions, still in denial. Through a fog I hear an officer say, "Mr. Philhower, do you know where Bryn Road is?"

My heart plummets. My blood runs chill. In an instant I know it's true. I fall apart.

Bryn Road is a winding and dangerous country road with no shoulders. It's one of a few ways to get to our neighborhood. I used to drive it with Cole before he had a driver's license. I would warn him, "Cole, do not ever drive this road when it's snowing or icy. *I* don't even drive on this road in those conditions. Take one of the other ways into the neighborhood."

At one section of the road you come down a hill that curves left. Straight ahead is a large oak tree, which sits eighteen inches off the road. Starting about fifty feet before the tree, just inches off the road, the ground slopes at a thirty-five-degree angle, then drops a few feet into a cornfield. If your tires leave the blacktop there, it's hard to wrestle your car back up because the slope pulls you down.

There is a large section of bark missing from the tree. I used to stop our car in front of it and say to Cole, "Look at the bark missing. Do you know why it's missing? Because of people hitting the tree with their car."

Cole had made another mark on that tree with his Jeep.

Cole had worked his shift at Jimmy John's, closed at 11:00 p.m., then went to hang out with his friend, Drew. He and Drew had been driving home at about 12:30 a.m. in the fog. The road was wet from rain. Cole's front tire had slid off the road about twenty-five feet in front of the tree. He had pulled hard to the left to correct, but it was in vain. The slope pulled him into the tree, which he couldn't see in the fog. There were no skid marks.

The tree is 1.3 miles from my driveway. Cole had driven that road hundreds of times. As many times as I had told Cole to never be on Bryn Road in snowy, icy conditions, the thought had never entered my mind to warn him about foggy and damp summer nights.

I hadn't seen Cole that morning, but I wasn't concerned. It was not uncommon for him to hang out with a friend, especially Drew, and then stay the night. Drew lived in our neighborhood and Cole and Drew had been friends since grade school. I had gone through my morning routine and left for work without thinking too much about it.

Somehow, through my fog of shock, I hear the officer say, "Do you know who Cole was with last night? There was another person in the car."

Could this nightmare possibly be even worse? "It was Drew," I murmur. "He was with Drew Dwyer last night."

They hadn't known who the other person was because Cole's Jeep had rolled down the hill into the cornfield, where it caught on fire and burst into flames. There was very little of the charred wreckage left and they had to use dental records to positively identify the boys. They have been putting together a list of potential friends who could have been with Cole so they can notify the other parents.

I'm completely numb. I'm still fighting reality. I call my mother and give her the news. My boss, John, and his boss, Tim, show up at Jen's house and find me pacing the sidewalk shaking, crying, and pleading out loud, "This can't be true!"

THE PH

There's nothing any of us can do. All I wan
go home, feel Cole's presence, and scream at the wan.
No one wants me to drive but I'm already in the car. Tim
jumps in the passenger seat to ride with me, with John
following behind.

I take Bryn Road. I pull up to the tree. The scene is
surreal. I see the new mark on the tree. The large burn
spot in the cornfield. I can't get out of my car. I drive off
babbling about how many times I had admonished Cole
and his friends to never drive on that road at night in
bad weather. But it was a summer night in June.

I pull into our development. Instead of turning left
onto my street, I drive straight ahead and pull up to the
Dwyers' house. Although I know Drew had been with
Cole, that hadn't been officially confirmed yet. Drew's
father, John, answers the doorbell and invites me in.

I say, "John, is Drew home?"

His answer is unclear.

I repeat, in a stern but shaky voice, "John, is Drew
home?"

With a stoic face, he says, "They are gone."

The police have already contacted the Dwyers.
He knows. We talk in a quiet state of shock for a few
minutes in their driveway.

John, Tim, and I leave and drive to my house. John
and Tim sit at my kitchen table while I lean against the
breakfast bar. I talk about how good our life was. I point
to a shoebox full of college recruiting letters on a desk.
We had so, so much more to do. They try to offer comfort.

I finally convince them to leave. I just need to look at
Cole's pictures and scream out loud.

Before I can do that the doorbell rings. It's one of Cole's friends, Chris. He shares a touching story about Cole with me, the first of what will be many I hear of things I never knew about Cole.

I thank Chris for stopping by. He leaves and I walk back to the kitchen. I receive a text from Jerod, one of Cole's lacrosse coaches. He was like a big brother to Cole and a second son to me. Cole was the little brother Jerod never had. They were great friends. He asks if he and Ryan, another coach, can come over and I say yes. They arrive and we cry together for an hour or so.

Then my door opens and in walks Traci, Tracy, and Colleen, friends who have sons who played lacrosse and were friends with Cole. They are carrying trays of sandwiches and bottled water and soda. This starts a nonstop flood of people coming over for the rest of the afternoon and evening. Personal friends, work friends, coaches, players, Cole's friends, parents, neighbors. I do my best to count as the evening goes on but I lose count at about eighty. It culminates with my mother and sister arriving at about 11 p.m. They have driven about seven hours to get here. I had no idea they were even coming.

I never get a chance to scream that night. But I do cry myself to sleep.

CHAPTER TWO

Live with No Regrets

"You only live once, but if you do it right,
once is enough." —*Mae West*

As I wake up the next morning, my first thought is, *Oh, God, it wasn't a dream.* This starts a pattern that will last for a couple of months: crying myself to sleep thinking, *What am I going to do?* — then waking up to the reality of, *It wasn't a dream.*

I begin another pattern that will last for the rest of the summer: Every day I drive to the high school and park my car in the same place I always did for all the years of watching Cole play sports and coaching. I walk the exact same path as always, a shortcut that takes me across the back of the south end zone. I never sat in the stands to watch Cole play; I preferred to stand on the sidelines just outside the coaches' box. So now I stand in the same place and yell the same things I always did: "Nice face off, Cole!" "Nice shot 49!" "Great defense, Cole!" "Great pass, 49!"

I stand on the field, stare up into the sky, and say three things: "Can you see me, bud? Do you know I still have your back? God, I want to see you again." Over time, I receive answers to my first two questions. The third statement is left hanging as a deep and inconsolable ache in my heart.

Then, after about forty-five minutes of being on the field, I drive to the site of the accident. Most times I see other people there, Cole's friends and other parents. For weeks, the vigils there last deep into the night. The county Sheriff's department have a squad there for many days and nights to help with traffic.

Days become weeks. Weeks become months. Months become years. And still, to this day, the deep ache remains.

Losing My World and Identity

For readers who never met Cole, how I wish you had the opportunity to know him. Cole was truly remarkable. He was wise beyond his years. He was a rock you could rely on. He was so much better than me in every way imaginable. If you were around Cole, you were a better person for it. He lit up the room and encouraged you just by being there.

Of course, I'm biased. But ask anyone who knew him and they'll all tell you the same things. As one of his high school teachers, Joe, wrote to me, "I don't recall Cole ever not being in a good mood. He always had a positive attitude. He was always so respectful of me and everyone else. He was always surrounded by friends—all kinds of friends! Cole's personality was infectious, and others gravitated toward him as a funny, clever, honest and hard-working kid who would be enjoyable to have on their team."

I wish I could truly convey to you the depth of my agony at the loss of my son and best friend. I wish I could convey to you how close we were. I can't say that we had the best father/son relationship in the world—but if there's a stronger, closer one, I just want to shake their hands. As my friend Colleen said to me through tears shortly after the accident, "When we heard about Cole, we all looked at each other and said, 'Why those two, God? Why did you break those two up?' You were a better father *and* mother to Cole than we are to our kids." She and the friends she was referring to are some of the best parents I've ever known, so this was one of the biggest compliments I've ever received.

After the accident, I've heard many stories of parents and children building better relationships as they saw Cole and I together. For example, my friend Dan, whose son Cam played lacrosse with Cole, told me, "Jim, you don't understand the impact you and Cole had on us. Watching you two changed my relationship with Cam forever." I had no idea. Other friends of Cole would openly tell me what Cole thought of our relationship from time to time. It confirmed what I knew.

The last time I saw Cole alive he was 6'1" and going on 200 pounds. The next time I saw him he was ashes in a small box. I lost not just Cole, but my entire identity. I lost the best job I will ever have: Cole's father. Cole was my whole world. Without Cole, I had no idea who I was, what the meaning of my life was, what I was going to do with my life. Learning to live without him has been indescribably difficult. I honestly don't know how I've done it so far.

I once received a compliment from a good friend, Wendy, who told me, "You've been an inspiration to us and the community. It's been incredible to watch you."

I thought, *Really?* Because I sure don't feel like an inspiration. Most times, I feel like I'm dragging the weight of the world around. People ask me, "How are you doing?" I usually answer with a typical, trite response, like, "One day at a time." The God's honest truth is that some days are very, very difficult, and most days are absolute hell. Christmastime is especially hard for me. Every year, when many of Cole's friends are home for the holidays, the thought hits me in full force, "You're never coming home to me again." I couldn't stand the thought of me not being there for Cole. It would have been so hard for him. The thought of him not being here for me never entered my mind.

One of the biggest things that has plagued me is the thought that Cole and I had so much left to do, and he had so much life left to live. College education (Cole was set on getting an MBA), college lacrosse, career, marriage, family—they are all gone now. I used to tell Cole, "My job is to see what you look like when you're twenty-five years old." That will never happen now.

I can't begin to describe to you how difficult the first year after Cole's accident was. It was a year of "firsts." The first time going to the grocery store without Cole, feeling like all eyes were on me. The first time going to work and coming home to an empty house. The first Thanksgiving, the first Christmas.

My first Father's Day without Cole was heartbreaking. When Cole was alive, Father's Day honestly wasn't that big of a deal for me. Since I heard, "I love you, Dad," "I appreciate you," "Thank you," pretty much every day, a special holiday wasn't necessary for us. We lived Father's Day every day. When Cole was younger, we would play golf on Father's Day morning, then watch the U.S. Open final in the afternoon. When Cole started traveling for Lacrosse, it seemed we were always finishing a tournament, then flying back home on Father's Day. I used to think, "There is *no* better way to spend a Father's Day weekend!"

But that first one without Cole really hurt. I still have the Father's Day card he gave me from the last year we were together. It sits in the same place and reads, "Thanks for all of the advice and support! Love Cole." That was lot of words for Cole on a card!

My house is well-built, but it's twenty-seven years old and dated in some areas. The kitchen was especially dated. We had a peninsula, which served as a breakfast bar, where Cole and I spent so much time together. It was a focal point of our lives. Cole ate most of his meals sitting on a stool at that peninsula. I'd often be talking to him on the other side. We discussed friends, girlfriends, sports, school, homework, business, politics, vacations, etc.

Cole and I had discussed remodeling the kitchen many times. But as much as we traveled for lacrosse, it just hadn't been a priority. The summer after Cole's death, I decided it was time to remodel. I knew how hard it would be to tear out that peninsula. As demolition day neared, it became harder and harder to face the thought of turning that space into open hardwood floor.

The remodel crew arrived right on time. I had taken many pictures of the kitchen to preserve memories. I had spent so much time looking over that peninsula and down at where Cole used to sit, closing my eyes and cherishing memories. Even still, I wasn't prepared for the pain and loss of breath I felt as demolition day arrived.

I spent that morning discussing details with the workers. I found myself walking behind the peninsula several times, putting my hands on it and looking down where Cole used to sit, walking around the various angles again and again. I must have walked into the laundry room on my way to the garage a half dozen times only to turn around and walk back in and look at it again. I asked the guys how much demolition would get done that day. They said most of the kitchen. I asked them if they could leave the peninsula just one more night. I'm sure they thought I was crazy, but they agreed.

I keep telling myself that Cole would have loved the kitchen remodel. I know he wouldn't miss the peninsula. But knowing that sure doesn't help. A day doesn't go by that I don't walk into my house from work and remember our times around the kitchen peninsula.

The lyrics of Kenny Chesney's song, "Who You'd Be Today" tear me up like you wouldn't believe:

Sunny days seem to hurt the most.
I wear the pain like a heavy coat.
I feel you everywhere I go.
I see your smile, I see your face,
I hear you laughin' in the rain.
I still can't believe you're gone.

It ain't fair: you died too young,
Like the story that had just begun,
But death tore the pages all away.
God knows how I miss you,
All the hell that I've been through,
Just knowin' no-one could take your place.
An' somctimes I wonder,
Who'd you be today?

Would you see the world? Would you chase your
dreams?
Settle down with a family,
I wonder what would you name your babies?
Some days the sky's so blue,
I feel like I can talk to you,
An' I know it might sound crazy.

Sunny days seem to hurt the most.
I wear the pain like a heavy coat.
The only thing that gives me hope,
Is I know I'll see you again someday.

As a parent, one of the hardest things about the loss
of a child is that you also lose control. You are no longer
there for them. It's not that our job as parents is to "fix"

things for our kids, but there's just nothing you can do to help them anymore when they're gone. It's such an indescribably painful feeling of helplessness and deep, permanent loss. I can't tell you how many times I've pleaded to God, "You took him—please take care of him! He is in your hands now."

About a year after Cole's death, his friends were home from school and I took several of them to Applebee's for a lunch on a Saturday afternoon. Seeing how much they had matured, physically, mentally, and emotionally, the thought hit me, "Do people age in heaven? When I see Cole again will I be talking to the same eighteen-year-old young man I knew so well? Or will he be different? Are there days in Heaven?" I don't know the answer to these questions. All I know is how much I miss him.

Continuing Cole's Legacy to Make a Difference

I can't get Cole back. I can't continue our life and finish everything we started. But I can do something to help others have a good life. I can build on Cole's legacy and do my best to inspire and uplift people, as he did when he was alive. This is why I'm writing this book—to somehow, in some small way, keep Cole's influence alive to make the world a better place, to inspire you to live your best life.

This book is organized into the following six parts, all of which reflect the influence Cole had on my life and that of others:

- Part I: Cultivate the Right Attitude
- Part II: Work Hard and Prepare

- Part III: Be a Good Teammate and Friend
- Part IV: Be a Servant Leader
- Part V: Enjoy Life by Being Present
- Part VI: Leave a Legacy

Cole was an exemplary individual from whom we can all learn in each of these areas. I hope you learn from him as you read his book. Throughout, I'll be sharing stories about Cole and relating them to your life.

A quick word on this: I sincerely hope my stories of Cole don't come across as typical father-son bragging, and I certainly don't mean to infer that Cole was so great because I was such a great father. When I say Cole was so much better than me, I really mean it. Cole was just naturally great. I may have provided guidance, but Cole earned every bit of praise he has received, both from me and everyone else who knew him. I learned so much from Cole, and I hope you do, too.

The title of this book comes from something I used to say to Cole. I never had to discipline Cole, and we never had a cross word (except for that time when he got a bad grade in Freshman Geometry). If Cole was not living up to his potential, for discipline the only thing I ever had to say to him was, "Is that the best you can do?" This was certainly not about shaming him, but rather simply a gentle and loving reminder. It's all I ever had to say. He immediately got it, and he would make whatever adjustments he needed to.

In continuing Cole's legacy, that's the question I want to gently ask all of us: *Is that the best you can do?*

It's the question I ask myself all the time to live up to what I tried to teach Cole all his life. It's a simple question, but if we really pause and think about it, it can be a profound help in our journey through life. It gives us space to pause and think about what's important, about whether or not we're being who we want to be.

You've Got One Shot, So Make It Count

Most importantly, "Is that the best you can do?" is a reminder to live with no regrets. Nothing makes you think about life more than the death of a loved one. We tend to go through life on autopilot, taking the most important things for granted. When those things are taken away, we often think regretfully, *I would have done things differently, had I known what I was going to lose.*

In that spirit, my message in this book to you is this: Make every moment count. Be present in each moment. Take nothing for granted. Live your best life. Live up to your full potential. Because you've only got one shot— and it may end far sooner than you imagine.

CHAPTER THREE

Yes, It Can Happen to You

"The saddest summary of a life contains
three descriptions: could have, might have,
and should have."

—*Louis E. Boone*

Cole and Drew passed away on June 27th, 2014. They were two of 451 car accident deaths in the state of Wisconsin in 2014.[1]

We read these types of statistics all the time. 610,000 Americans die from heart attacks every year, which is one in every four deaths.[2] Each minute, someone in the United States dies from a heart disease-related event.[3] For American males, the average lifetime risk of developing some form of cancer is 40.8 percent, or a little less than a one in two chance.[4] Each year, 136,053 Americans are killed in accidents, 93,541 die from Alzheimer's disease,

76,488 die from diabetes, and 55,227 die from influenza and pneumonia.[5]

Here's the thing: These are all just statistics, just abstract numbers—until it happens to someone you love. Then, it's not just a number. It's a human being—a mother or father, son or daughter, brother or sister, grandparent, friend, teacher. Each number represents a human life who touched other lives. It's a person who was here one moment, and gone the next. It's a person with dreams and goals that will never be realized, gifts and talents that will no longer be utilized. It's deeds left undone, words left unsaid. It's a gaping, aching hole that's left in the hearts of everyone close to him or her.

We read these statistics, these meaningless numbers on paper, and, without thinking much about it, just assume that it can't happen to us. "My mother can't be diagnosed with cancer." "My father won't die until he's 100." "My wife won't die of a heart attack." "My son won't die in a car accident." Until it does happen to us. Then, all those unspoken, subconscious assumptions explode as our hearts are ripped from our chests.

It can happen to any one of us at any time. There's no guarantee that a loved one of yours won't die in the time it takes you to read this sentence. There's no guarantee that it can't happen to *you*—today, tomorrow, any day. Look around you. Appreciate what you have. Nothing will be the same in a year.

I wish I could inject this sentiment into your veins: *Never take a moment with a loved one for granted. Never take a single breath for granted.* This moment, right here, right now, is a gift, a miracle. Pause for a moment. Look around you. Look at the sights, the colors, the abundance that surrounds you. Feel your body, your hands and fingers, your feet and toes. Breathe into your lungs and feel the sensation of your breath.

Think of the people whom you love the most. Envision their smiles and laughs. Think of the kind words they've spoken to you, moments of connection. Think of your fondest memories, the experiences that have shaped your life and brought you joy.

Now ponder on these questions:

- What would life be like without sight or hearing, without arms or legs? What would life be like if I were paralyzed?
- What would life be like without _____ (your favorite person in the world)?
- What would my life have been like had I been born in another country, to a different family?
- What am I most grateful for? What if these things were to disappear?

This life is so hard. We all experience so much pain. Yet it is also so wondrous, beautiful, and full of joy. And it is oh, so short.

Your life and the people in it are not just numbers or statistics. You were born for a purpose. No one else sees the world quite like you see it, no one else can give the world what you have to offer. No other human being who has ever walked the earth experiences life in quite the same way as you.

Don't ever forget that. As you go about your daily life, keep in remembrance the gift of each breath, each moment. As you read statistics and watch the news, remember this: It happened to us, and *it can happen to you at any time.* Everything can change in the blink of an eye. So forgive often and love with all your heart. You never know when you may never have that chance again.

Focus on the Most Important Things

In our desire to make the most of our life, we often become overly ambitious and accomplishment-driven. Unfortunately, this can create a scenario where, in our drive to become someone and accomplish great things, we miss out on the simple and most important things. Please understand that when I encourage you to live with no regrets, this is not what I'm speaking of. I'm talking about always understanding what the most important things are, and living accordingly.

Bronnie Ware is an Australian nurse who cares for people in the last few weeks of their lives. Her experience sheds a lot of light on how to live with no regrets. She interviewed her patients and asked them what they regretted most about their lives. The most common responses she received, which she expounds on in her book, *The Top Five Regrets of the Dying*, were,

1. "I wish I'd had the courage to live a life true to myself, not the life others expected of me."
2. "I wish I didn't work so hard."
3. "I wish I'd had the courage to express my feelings."
4. "I wish I had stayed in touch with my friends."
5. "I wish I had let myself be happier."

Karl Pillemer is an American gerontologist who studies the changes people experience as they age. His research also adds to this discussion. He asked more than 1,200 seniors, "Over the course of your life, what are the most important lessons you would like to pass on to younger people?" From those responses, he wrote his book, *30 Lessons for Living: Tried and True Advice from the Wisest Americans.* Here are the top ten responses that emerged:

1. Choose a career for the intrinsic rewards, not the financial ones.
2. Act now like you will need your body for a hundred years.
3. Take a risk and a leap of faith when opportunity knocks.
4. Choose a mate with extreme care.
5. Travel more.
6. Don't wait to say words that need to be said, such as "I'm sorry," "Thank you," "I love you."
7. Time is of the essence: Live as though life is short—because it is.
8. Happiness is a choice, not a condition.
9. Time spent worrying is time wasted: Stop worrying.
10. When it comes to making the most of your life, think small. Savor the simple daily pleasures.

Thankfully, I can honestly say that I have no regrets about my life with Cole. I don't say this to brag, by any means. I'm just so grateful that we made the most of our time together.

The last words I said to Cole, as he was leaving for work the night of the accident, were, "I love you, bud. Be proud of your work."

His last words to me in response were, "Love you, dad."

If there's any solace for me in Cole's death, at least I can say I wouldn't have changed anything about how he was raised or the time I spent with him. I fully lived and loved every minute of it.

I hope to God that you don't have to go through a heart-wrenching tragedy to learn these lessons. My hope is that you will learn from my experience and the lessons in this book to make your life as fulfilling as it can be. Because nothing hurts worse than the pain of regret.

CHAPTER FOUR

We Need the Clichés

"Success is simple. You know what's right and you know what's wrong. Do what's right."

—Jim Philhower

As the Director of North America Sales and Leadership Development for Henry Schein, a Fortune 200 company, I do a lot of speaking and training for our sales teams and dentists. But for many years I've had the itch to speak to high school students.

A few years ago, when Cole was in high school, I walked into our living room and Cole was sitting on the couch, playing with his phone. I said, "Hey bud, here's dad's latest idea."

He looked up at me, put his phone down, and said, "Okay, what?"

I said, "I want to speak in high schools one day." He bit his lower lip and had his familiar cocked grin on his face that I knew so well. "What do you think, bud?" I asked.

He said, "Great idea, dad. Just as soon as I graduate."

We had a good laugh over that. The truth is that he would have been proud of me for doing it. He was just busting his old man.

I once took Cole to a business function where I was speaking, and a colleague of mine asked him, "Have you ever heard your dad speak?"

Cole answered, grinning, "I live it every day."

Cole was always getting an earful from me. I tried to teach him life lessons at every opportunity. He might have razzed me about it, but I know he appreciated it.

The more I was around Cole's friends and other kids from junior high to high school, the more I realized that many parents didn't talk to their kids in the same way I did with Cole. I'm not saying my way was perfect, but I just know that many of these kids didn't hear some of the same messages that Cole grew up hearing. And even if they were hearing it, teenagers often ignore their parents and need to hear it from someone else. So I thought it would be pretty cool if I could speak to kids and inspire them, somehow make a difference in their lives.

About a year after Cole's death, I was invited to speak at a program called "Life of an Athlete," which was open to all athletes, including the lacrosse team, at Kettle Moraine High School, where Cole had graduated. That never would have happened if Cole had still been alive. Cole would have moved on and I would have been chasing him around the country watching him play college lacrosse.

My presentation was entitled, "Your Free Ticket to Success." I told them that what I would share with them would cost them nothing, but would be absolutely critical to their success in life, in any career or endeavor—and, they're the things that most people screw up the most. I taught them simple things like respect, courtesy, saying "thank you," character, teamwork, commitment, honesty, hard work, and goal-setting. There was nothing particularly earth-shaking or mind-blowing—it was just the simple, common-sense attributes that make all the difference in life. When applied, they're guaranteed to increase your chances of success. When ignored, they are guaranteed to hold you back.

This is what you'll find in this book. The truth is, I just don't know how to make it complicated. Success may not be easy, but the formula is simple. It's so simple that it can seem like a cliché.

But I urge you to pay attention as you read this book. What you'll learn may be simple. You may think you've heard it before. But success principles become clichés precisely because *they work*. They are the tried-and-true wisdom of the ages: Treat others with respect, even if you have nothing to gain from them. You choose your attitude. Be proud of your work. There are no shortcuts in life. You have to prepare to win. Unsuccessful people have an attitude of entitlement; successful people have an attitude of gratitude. If it is to be, it's up to me. There's never a traffic jam on the extra mile.

We're losing many of these clichés in our culture, the more we shift to a culture of blame and entitlement. We could all use a solid dose of plain-spoken, homespun common sense, however cliché it may seem. Social critics, intellectuals, and pundits make everything so complicated. But underlying all the complexities of life are basic, simple principles for success that we ignore to our peril.

Death has a way of reminding us of all the little things we take for granted so easily. My intention in this book isn't to give you anything new or revolutionary. Rather, it is to give you a gentle reminder of the things that should be second nature to all of us but seem to have been lost. These are the things we have to keep coming back to, over and over again, throughout our individual lives and in our cultural cycles.

Cole heard these things throughout his entire life. More importantly, he exemplified them—which was more due to his nature than my teaching. To honor Cole, I want to teach you what he knew and lived, and what I learned from him. Because the truth is this: Every truly successful person who has ever lived has become so by consistently living the clichés. My hope is that, in the context of Cole's death, the proven clichés of successful living will come alive for you.

PART I

Cultivate the Right Attitude

Winston Churchill nailed it when he said, "Attitude is a little thing that makes a big difference." I call "attitude" the magic word, because nothing influences our success more than our attitude—and nothing is easier to manage.

Have you ever looked at someone and thought, "Why are they so lucky? Things just come easy to them. They never seem to have major issues"?

If you take a closer look, you'll find that it's not that they don't have problems—we all do—but rather that they have a good attitude when they encounter them. They have a positive outlook on life. They're fun people to be around. They're grateful for where they are and what they have in life, not pessimistic and constantly complaining about the world. They expect good things to happen, and they usually do. Like a mirror image, the world tends to give us back exactly what we give out.

Everyone experiences challenges. The difference in these people is they don't let those situations keep them down. And they certainly don't spend half their time telling anyone who will listen how bad things are.

Our attitude is contagious. We have to ask ourselves, though, "Is it worth catching?" We choose our attitude every day, and in every circumstance. We choose whether to focus on the negative or the positive. We choose every day whether things will help us or hinder us, whether we will be part of the problem or part of the solution, whether we will drag others down or uplift them.

One of the things I appreciated most about Cole was his attitude. I may have taught him the importance of attitude in words, but he showed me its importance in his actions. In this section, we'll learn from Cole and others how to cultivate the right attitude for success.

CHAPTER FIVE

If It Is to Be, It's Up to Me

Caesar Barber didn't want to die. So he filed a lawsuit. Barber, a maintenance supervisor, weighs 272 pounds. He has diabetes and high blood pressure and cholesterol, and he suffered two heart attacks before the age of fifty-six.

Barber's health problems, he claimed in his lawsuit, were caused by fast-food corporations. He said, "I trace [my health problems] back to the high fat, grease and salt, all back to McDonald's, Wendy's, Burger King—there was no fast food I didn't eat, and I ate it more often than not because I was single, it was quick, and I'm not a very good cook. It was a necessity, and I think it was killing me, my doctor said it was killing me, and I don't want to die."[6]

Keith Brown would undoubtedly sympathize with Barber. An inmate in an Idaho prison, Brown filed suit against several national beer and wine companies, blaming them for the almost thirty years he has spent in prison. Alcohol, he says, has "played a major role" in the crimes that landed him there. He stated in his self-drafted lawsuit that, "At no time in my life, prior to me becoming an alcoholic, was I ever informed that alcohol was habit forming and addictive."[7]

Perhaps Bernard Bey, a thirty-two-year-old homeless Brooklyn man, was trying to one-up Barber and Brown when he filed a lawsuit against his parents, stating that they have been "indifferent" to his "problems." Blaming them for his homelessness and aimlessness, he said, "I feel abandoned. The relationship I share with my parents is not a beneficial one. Not a loving, nurturing one...Their actions over the years have caused deep rooted wounds that cannot heal on their own."[8]

Apparently, those wounds can be healed by the $200,000 he wants a judge to force his parents to pay him.

"If you could kick the person in the pants responsible for most of your trouble, you wouldn't sit for a month." —*Theodore Roosevelt*

We can snicker at the blatant absurdity of Barber, Brown, and Bey. But by doing so, we miss a critical lesson:

Every one of us shares their tendencies. I don't highlight them to mock them, but rather to learn from them.

Too many people look for someone else to blame for their failures and inadequacies. In one form or another, to one degree or another, our natural human tendency is to try to escape responsibility. Our irresponsibility and victimhood may not be as extreme as theirs, but it still cripples and limits us.

> "It's not what happens to you that determines how far you will go in life; it is how you handle what happens to you." —*Zig Ziglar*

Every time we get angry at the person who cuts us off on the freeway, we're playing the role of the victim. As long as we harbor wounds and refuse to forgive our parents for hurting us, we remain in victim mode. Even worse is blaming people from generations earlier.

The irony is that we blame others in an attempt to fix things, but by so doing, we eliminate our ability to fix anything. We all have the power to change our life through our choices. But we often relinquish our power through victimhood. The only way to reclaim our power is through personal responsibility.

It seems more so today than ever that people have a victim mentality. People think someone owes them something, they deserve more, others have prospered disproportionally, the government should do more for them, etc. This victim mentality is perpetuated a lot in the media. Until we overcome it fully, we have no power to change our lives.

Personal Responsibility: The Foundation of a Successful Attitude

Thankfully, I had great parents who raised me to take responsibility for my choices and results. I learned from them the principle that, "If it is to be, it's up to me." I learned from them that the foundation of a healthy, productive attitude is personal responsibility—taking ownership for your life.

I started working at a young age. My family owned a drug store in Dayton, Ohio. I started working there, packing boxes downstairs, and sorting shipments. But I wanted to be independent of that, so I looked for other places to work. Cole used to hate this story because he heard it so often: One of my earliest memories of earning money is working for a next-door neighbor who had a small farm when I was about ten years old. One day I helped him bale hay and put it up in his barn. He paid me a penny a bale. We put up about 700 bales of hay that day, and he gave me $7. I thought I was rich!

My parents divorced when I was sixteen years old. When I was eighteen, my father was killed in a car accident, just a few miles from our home. I was there when they used the "jaws of life" to cut the car open and found him dead.

I didn't have a choice but to own my life and work hard. My younger brother and sister went to live with my mom, but I chose to stay in my dad's house, where we grew up. I damn sure couldn't afford it, but I was determined to keep it. It wasn't a massive house—just a typical 1970's bi-level. It was in and out of foreclosure several times, but somehow I managed to hang onto it.

"People are always blaming their circumstances for what they are. I don't believe in circumstances. The people who get on in this world are the people who get up and look for the circumstances they want, and if they can't find them, make them." —*George Bernard Shaw*

One time the propane tank, which ran my heater and water heater, ran out of fuel in the middle of winter. I barely scraped together $50, which was lot of money for an eighteen-year-old kid in 1980. I called George Kuhn, the owner of the propane delivery company, and asked him if he could send a truck out and give me $50 worth of propane.

He responded, "I can't make any money doing that. I can't send a man to your house at $15 an hour in a $25,000 truck for $50."

So I had to bundle up and take cold showers until I could save up enough for him to fill the tank. I remember being pretty cold for a couple of weeks. I slept under blankets five layers deep because I could see my frozen breath in the house.

I never went to college. I was thrust into adult life too soon, and I had to hustle to make a living. The only thing I had going for me was desire and worth ethic. I really had no choice but to have a good attitude. There was no one who could bail me out.

I learned really quickly that it's not what you have that matters—it's what you *do* with what you have. What matters isn't what happens to you, but rather how you respond to what happens. You play the hand you're dealt, and you don't whine about it.

"Hardships often prepare ordinary people for an extraordinary destiny." —*C.S. Lewis*

Embracing the Joy of Response-Ability

When I say "responsibility," clue into how that word feels to you. For most people, it conjures feelings of blame, shame, and pain. It feels like a burden. Subconsciously, it has a dark and heavy feel to it.

We cringe at hearing "It's your responsibility" because what we really hear is, "It's your fault. You are to blame."

But let's take another look at the word "responsibility" to see if we can change our orientation to it. Break the word down and we find "response" plus "ability." In other words, responsibility simply means having the ability to respond.

Responsibility is our ability to choose our actions and responses to anything that happens to us. It is our ability to choose how we spend our time and energy. It is our ability to create different outcomes. As Viktor Frankl discovered in a Nazi concentration camp, "Everything can be taken from a man but one thing: the last of the human freedoms—to choose one's attitude in any given set of circumstances, to choose one's own way."

Reclaiming Our Power

Responsibility is not a blaming or shameful word, but rather an empowering word.

Responsibility, when properly understood, is one of the most exciting, powerful, and joyful principles we have to create our ideal lives.

The people who take the least responsibility for their circumstances and results have the least power and ability to improve them. Likewise, those who take the most responsibility have the greatest power and ability to improve their circumstances and results.

Until we accept responsibility, we have no power to change anything because we have no power over our circumstances. If we didn't cause something, then there's nothing we can do to fix it. But if we see how we are the owners of our feelings and results, we have the power to change them. The point of taking responsibility isn't to increase our burden of shame, but simply to make our lives better. We are much more a product of our decisions than our circumstances.

"If you own this story, you get to write the ending." —*Brené Brown*

45

Achieve Excellence Through Adversity

In Cole's junior year of lacrosse, he was the obvious choice to be a team captain. That's not just me saying that—talk to any of his teammates and their parents and they'll agree. Everyone just expected it. But that year he had a new head coach, who for whatever reason decided to choose other captains. That was hard for both me and Cole to accept, although I think I took it harder than Cole.

Traditionally, lacrosse teams have three captains. This coach chose to go with only two seniors. He told Cole that the reason why he chose them was because he wanted seniors as captains. The next year, however, when Cole was a senior, he passed over Cole again and chose a senior and a junior as captains. Cole wasn't the only person shocked and disappointed by the decision. The team was embarrassed for Cole and ticked off at the coach. There was a lot of private grumbling in the ranks about the coach over that decision. One of Cole's friends, Trevor, was chosen as one of the captains. He told me, "It was honestly embarrassing. Everyone knew Cole was the hardest working kid on the team and our leader."

But Cole took it in stride and never once complained about it. He and that coach didn't really gel, but he never once talked back. In fact, one time I asked Cole about it and he stopped me cold and said, "Dad, we're done talking about it. Every kid on that team knows who our team leader is. When it's crunch time in a crucial game, I know who they're looking to for leadership." It was such a rarity for Cole to talk to me like that—usually he was open to anything I had to say. But he was right, and he never said another word about it. He took responsibility for what he could control—his attitude and efforts—and went to work. His efforts paid off: By the end of the season, he had been made a team captain.

Achieving personal excellence doesn't just happen—it's a choice. It's a decision you make or fail to make. But in the absence of your commitment to excellence, you default to average, or worse, mediocrity.

"Any fact facing us is not as important as our attitude toward it, for that determines our success or failure. The way you think about a fact may defeat you before you ever do anything about it. You are overcome by the fact because you think you are." —*Norman Vincent Peale*

When Cole was a young player, his travel team, who were among the best players in the state of Wisconsin, played a tournament in Maryland. (The east coast is the most popular place in the country and the best competition for lacrosse.) To put it bluntly, they got their butts kicked, and soundly. Most games weren't even a contest, and they only won two. They lost one game 12 to 1. Some of the kids on the team were even crying.

Another of Cole's coaches, Paul, told me of that experience, "Cole was maybe one of five kids who came back and learned something from it. He accepted that they weren't as good as they thought they were. He took that lesson to heart and put the work in. From that tournament until he graduated, Cole was the best player and had the best attitude of anyone on the team."

~~~~~~~~~~~~~~~~~~~~~~~~~~~~~~

"Circumstances do not make the man, they merely reveal him to himself." *–Epictetus*

~~~~~~~~~~~~~~~~~~~~~~~~~~~~~~

Cole's travel team got much better and made several east coast trips over the ensuing years. They became competitive against the best teams on the east coast. (In fact, because of how much he played with travel teams and college recruiting camps, Cole played more games outside of the state of Wisconsin than he did in-state even though he played four years of varsity.)

When disappointing things happen to us, we can get bitter or we can get better. Cole always chose the latter. And anyone who does so finds that they have much greater power and control over their experience and results in life.

CHAPTER SIX

The Best Players Play

~~~~~~~~~~~~~~~~~~~~~~~~~~~~~~

"Success is not an entitlement.
It has to be earned." —*Howard Shultz*

~~~~~~~~~~~~~~~~~~~~~~~~~~~~~~

All college coaches must be reading from the same handbook. Cole got the same answer every time he asked the question.

During Cole's college recruiting process, several collegiate lacrosse programs reached out to recruit him. So we spent a lot of time touring campuses and visiting with coaches. Every time the tour was done, there would be a private conversation between us and the head coach. I would let Cole do all the talking and I would just sit there and listen. I wanted him to own the experience and his decision.

Cole would ask questions about what offense and defense they ran to learn how well he'd fit into their system. Inevitably, at some point in the conversation the real question would come out: "Hey, Coach, how much playing time do you think I'll get?"

Every coach we ever sat with—and there were a few—had the same response, in so many words: "Cole, you'll have every opportunity to not only play as a freshman, but to be on the starting front line as a freshman. The best players play. Any other questions?"

I got a kick out of that. And I loved the lesson it taught to Cole: You'll have equal opportunity to play, but you're not entitled to anything. You have to earn your way to the top.

Entitlement: The Poison of Success

Nothing kills success like a sense of entitlement—the belief that we deserve everything to go our way, the idea that the world somehow owes us something. One informational website lists "sense of entitlement" as a personality disorder, and defines it as, "An unrealistic, unmerited or inappropriate expectation of favorable living conditions and favorable treatment at the hands of others."[9]

Entitled people fall into the trap of victimhood every time they feel they are wronged by life, circumstance, or other people. They feel sorry for themselves, and they make this known in melodramatic ways. They take what they have for granted and rarely feel a full sense of gratitude.

They impose demands on others, then throw tantrums whenever their demands aren't met. They'll do anything and everything to get what they think they deserve, even if it comes at the expense of others.

They tear others down to build themselves up. They tend to be super competitive, rather than cooperative, with others. They look out for themselves first and foremost, and rarely consider the needs of others. They take more than they give. They demand respect without giving it in return. They don't consider how their actions affect others.

"When we replace a sense of service and gratitude with a sense of entitlement and expectation, we quickly see the demise of our relationships, society, and economy."

—*Steve Maraboli*

Success Must Be Earned

The problem with all of these symptoms of entitlement is that it simply prevents us from achieving our goals. The selfishness it creates pushes people away from us. It prevents us from learning and growing because, when we point fingers of blame, we're not turning inward to take personal responsibility.

We can't change anything if we're not responsible, and we'll never be responsible if we're entitled. The more we expect the government or others to give us something we feel we are entitled to, the less responsible we are for our lives. This gets in the way of our own empowerment and achievement. The reality is that none of us are entitled to anything. Success is not given, but rather earned. All of us must pay the price.

Sadly, while coaching and watching sports with Cole for many years, I saw a lot of entitlement. For example, some parents would go nuts because their kid was a superstar in a youth league or on JV, and when they got to varsity they didn't play as much. I kid you not, I've literally seen parents in the stands holding stopwatches, timing exactly how much playing time their son or daughter got.

But just as Cole learned, no one is entitled to playing time on varsity. At the varsity level, we need to win games. It's not a participation sport. The best players play. It's that simple. If you want to play, you have to improve your game. You have to stop bitching about all the things you can't control—the coach, the players, the refs, etc.—and focus on what you can control: your attitude and effort.

And I've been on both sides of this: Cole played on varsity all four years in high school and was a starter for three of those years, but he also rode the bench in other sports in junior high. Sure, there have been times when I've been frustrated and wished Cole was getting more playing time. So I'd work with him to see what we needed to do to improve his game. He took advantage of every opportunity and earned his playing time, and he never took it for granted.

There are no trophies for simply participating in life (breathing). Whatever we want in life, we have to earn. Athletes are not entitled to be on varsity just because they were great in youth. They're not entitled to more playing time over someone else just because they feel like they deserve it. Students are not entitled to a better grade when they don't put in the effort to get it.

Our personal issues aren't other people's problems. When I speak to high school students I always say, "Let me know how it goes for you when you tell your college professors that you need that better grade when you haven't put forth the effort. Let me know how it goes for you when you tell your boss that you're entitled to that raise or promotion when you didn't earn it." A lot of entitled youth are in for a rude awakening when they get into the adult world. And sadly, this sense of entitlement follows many people into adulthood.

Here's what we're entitled to: We're entitled to an opportunity each and every day to improve our character, education, and skills. We're entitled to make a difference in society, to make our communities better. We're entitled to take responsibility for our attitude, choices, and results. We are entitled to give back and increase our contributions daily. Your success in life will be in direct relationship to your contributions to society.

Cole's Work Ethic

Cole and I lived a comfortable upper-middle-class life. He never wanted for anything. I taught him the value of work, but I didn't have to require him to work because he always wanted to. He didn't need the money, but he chose to work from a young age.

I'll never forget the time when he was about eleven years old, and he and Drew decided to start a little business washing cars in the neighborhood. I had nothing to do with it, and I didn't even know they were doing it. The two of them initiated and followed through on the whole thing. They went out and started knocking on doors in our neighborhood and asking, "Would you like to have your car washed?"

If anyone said yes, they would respond, "You got a bucket, soap, and a rag we can use? And can we use your hose?" Apparently, they were strong on initiation, and a bit weak on the preparation. Together, they made $120 that first day and split it evenly. Cole came home with $60 and told me what they had done. I still crack up every time I think of that.

Cole was always looking for ways to make money, even long before he could drive. He would mow the neighbors' lawns, work for local farmers, whatever he could find. There's a doctor who lives down the road from us and he hired a few boys for summer work. Cole did a lot of work for him between ten and fourteen years old. He didn't invite many of the kids back because they didn't work hard enough. But Cole always got an invitation to come back. He got his first formal W-2 job as soon as he turned sixteen, and he always had a job after that.

And when he wasn't working at his job, he was hustling some deal. I didn't know a lot about all his side deals. At his funeral, one of his best friends, Jake Miller, gave a eulogy in which he said, "Talking about business plans was part of his everyday routine. He constantly looked for ways to manage his money, manage his time, and become the most successful businessman in the world. He could achieve anything he set his mind to."

Later, I asked Jake, "What are these business plans of Cole's you were talking about?" He responded, "Mr. Philhower, Cole always had something going on."

He would save his money to buy something, which he could then trade for something else. He was always listing things for sale on Craigslist. One Saturday, when he was about fourteen, he told me, "Dad, I've got someone coming over here." It was some guy, about twenty-six years old, who had read his Craigslist ad. They were trading headphones or something. I let Cole do all the talking because he could always handle himself, no matter the age difference.

My point is that Cole just naturally got that he wasn't entitled to anything. He worked hard for everything. He never took anything for granted. He was such a great example to me.

Gratitude: The Antidote of Entitlement

Here's the plain truth: Life just ain't fair. We can deny it. We can whine about it. We can fight against it. But nothing changes that fact. Lots of stuff happens that we're not prepared for, that takes the wind out of our sails, that brings us to our knees in agony. That's the way it goes. We can complain about all the things we don't have and all the things that didn't go our way, or we can be grateful for everything we have and all our experiences. The choice is ours.

Successful people have an attitude of gratitude, unsuccessful people have an attitude of entitlement. Nothing dissolves entitlement like gratitude.

Gratitude has the power to transform all negative thoughts, emotions, perceptions, and experiences into positive, uplifting, joyful ones. Gratitude gives us more compassion and love, because as we realize how blessed we are, we want to give to others. Gratitude makes us see negative experiences with new eyes, improves our physical health, and expands our energy. Gratitude is the candle that shines through our darkest moments, blessing us with hope, drawing forth our faith.

Cole was such a grateful person, and it served him well in his life. I never heard him complain about something he didn't have, and he expressed gratitude all the time, even from a young age. It served him well in life.

It's been my experience that some people who have it all and enjoy so many luxuries tend to complain about the pettiest things. In my experience, the people who have never had to suffer much tend to be less grateful than others. Gratitude doesn't just happen—it's a conscious choice, and it must be cultivated.

In sports and in life, the best players play. And the best players tend to be those who have an attitude of gratitude, rather than an attitude of entitlement. The same is true for those who are successful in life.

CHAPTER SEVEN

Respect Matters

~~~~~~~~~~~~~~~~~~~~~~~~~~~

*"I speak to everyone in the same way,
whether he is the garbage man or the president
of the university." —Albert Einstein*

~~~~~~~~~~~~~~~~~~~~~~~~~~~

Joe Amplo is the head coach for the Marquette University men's lacrosse team. He's a big name in the sport, and very well respected. One time he came and delivered a presentation to Cole's state travel team when Cole was a sophomore.

I remember much of what he said. But one thing really stood out to me. Speaking of what he looks for in recruits, he said, "I can get great lacrosse players. They're a dime a dozen. I have lots to choose from, and there are only so many college lacrosse programs to play for. So great players are just a given. What I'm really looking for are kids who are going to represent Marquette University the way we want to be represented.

"I'm looking for the kid who treats the gate agent at the airport well. The kid who will stand up and help the lady put her bag in the overhead compartment. The kid who will treat the janitor with as much respect as he treats me."

He continued to explain that he often won't wear Marquette gear on recruiting trips because he doesn't want people to recognize him. It allows him to observe how kids act when they don't know who he is. He said, "I want to see how they're interacting with and treating other people."

One of the most important attributes of a good attitude is respect. A little respect goes a long way to opening doors and creating opportunities, forging friendships, and endearing people to us.

Hire Character, Train Skill

What Coach Amplo was teaching was something I learned in business a long time ago: Hire character, and train skill. Skills are so much easier to coach than respect and character.

If a person hasn't learned respect and hasn't developed their character at a young age, it's not likely that they'll learn it when they're older. And it's nearly impossible to instill character, respect, and a good attitude in people. If you've ever worked in a service position, have you ever served someone who was a jerk? I can guarantee that this person was a jerk in high school. They just grew up to be a bigger jerk later in life. People don't hit age thirty-five and suddenly decide to be jerks. Either no one taught them or they simply didn't learn basic rules of civility.

There are plenty of people who are willing to work hard to develop their skills in order to compete, whether in sports or careers. But it's surprising how few people are willing to learn basic courtesy and cultivate respect. If you want a successful career, if you want to reach your goals, you have to learn how to treat people with respect. It's such a basic, fundamental thing, yet it's incredibly rare.

As you're building up your resume and seeking to advance your career, never forget this principle. Develop your skills, to be sure, but also focus on treating others with more respect. Furthermore, never be intimidated by any job because you lack experience or skills. Compensate for any such lack with an abundance of respect and you'll be surprised at how far that can take you.

The foundation of character is honesty, which Cole had in abundance. One time he was working as a busser for a local brew house. A family had leftover pizza and he asked them if they wanted him to box it up. They said yes, so he carried their pizza into the kitchen. Just as he was walking through the door of the kitchen, one of his co-workers bumped into him. He dropped the pizza and several of the pieces hit the floor.

It would have been easy for him to just box it up and not say a word. But he threw away the pizza that had hit the floor. There was maybe one or two pieces left. He took what was left back to the table and said, "I'm really sorry, but I dropped your pizza and most of it hit the floor. This is all that's left."

The guy smiled and said, "Thanks for being honest. No worries." And he gave Cole a big tip just for being honest.

Honesty will take you much farther in life than skill.

Respect is About Humility

Respect is measured by how well we treat people who are weaker than us and from whom we have nothing to gain. Respectful people never put themselves above anyone. True respect isn't about condescending and being "nice" to people "below" us—it's about not seeing ourselves as above anyone in the first place. I have worked with and seen many people who manage "up" very well, but do not manage "down" well. In other words, they show a lot of deference for their bosses, but not so much for subordinates.

When I'm considering prospects for sales positions, I want to know how they treat the receptionist when they come in for an interview. How do they treat service technicians they bump into in the parking lot? If they don't demonstrate courtesy and respect—particularly to people in perceived "lesser" positions—it's an automatic ticket out.

I coach and speak to a lot of dentists, and one of the things I teach is how to hire the right people. I coach doctors that, once they have their candidates narrowed down to a final two or three, then have the team take them out to lunch—without the doctor. Observe how they treat the wait staff, their table manners, their casual conversation. You want to see how they naturally and instinctively behave and treat people whom they have no reason to impress.

This is one of the things I loved most about Cole. After the accident, so many people came forward with stories of how well he treated people, especially the disadvantaged. Cole had an eclectic group of friends. It didn't matter to Cole if you were the biggest star athlete, the valedictorian, or a challenged kid—he embraced everyone and treated everyone the same.

One of Cole's friends, whom I never would have known had it not been for the accident, was a challenged young man with Asperger's. With tears in his eyes, he told me, "Mr. P, if you could just sit at the lunch table with Cole, you knew you fit it in." Another of Cole's friends, Chris, is also challenged and is often the target of kids picking on him. He came to my house the day of the accident and told me about an encouraging text he had once received from Cole. He told me that he read the text daily and used it for motivation. It had meant so much to him, coming from Cole.

One of Cole's coaches, Dave, told me about a time when their team dominated their opponent and beat them by many goals. He noticed Cole approach the opposing team's goalie as he was walking to the team bus. Cole put his arm around his shoulder and spoke with him for a few minutes. When Cole came back to his team, Dave asked him what he had said to the goalie. He had told him that he had played a good game and to not let this lopsided victory discourage him for the rest of the season. Dave told me, "This is not something that high school players do—especially to the players of opposing teams! It's normally left up to the coaches to lift the morale of their own players. This showed Cole's character, not only as an athlete, but as a caring individual."

One of Cole's friends, Luc, told me how inclusive Cole was in everything they did, and how he made everyone feel welcome and comfortable. He spoke of how Cole was always organizing informal practices and inviting everyone and anyone, regardless of their skill level. Luc, who was a year older than Cole and an excellent player as well, said, "A lot of guys were very particular about who they let play, but Cole didn't care. Cole wanted everyone to play. If you were with Cole, you just knew that no one would be excluded. He never made you feel like, 'Oh man, Cole's too good for me to play with him,' or anything like that. Cole was always very open to any level of player. It wasn't just about winning for him. That's why he was the leader."

When we treat everyone with respect, regardless of his or her station in life, we create a safe place for people. Others are drawn to us because of how we make them feel. Respect is about seeing the best in others, and when we do that, we inspire them to live up to their full potential.

Respect is About Noticing the Little Things

When I speak to high school students, I often ask them, "When was the last time you said 'thank you' to your parents—and not just for those jeans that you 'had to have'? Do you thank them for the food they prepare for you, the clothes they wash for you? What about all the daily routines of putting your needs first? Do you notice how food magically appears in the refrigerator? How you always seem to have money in your school lunch account? Notice and thank them for all those little things they do for you every day so that your life goes smoother."

Of course, this doesn't just apply to youth. As adults, a lot of people do little things for us all the time. Do we notice when our clothes get laundered and our dishes get washed? Do we notice how shiny the janitor makes the floor? Do we notice when someone makes coffee? Do we notice when our kids clean their rooms or do their homework without being asked?

The more we tune into the little things and express gratitude for them, the more respect becomes a natural, habitual part of our lives. I don't believe we can consistently act one way in private and another way in public. We are what we repeatedly do.

I was taught to always say "Yes, sir," and "Yes, ma'am" to everyone I'm speaking with. To shake hands with a firm grip and look people in the eye. To thank people for their service. To sit up straight. To be polite. I always taught Cole to do the same. These aren't big things. They're simple. But when we make them habits, we really stand out.

It's one of the many reasons Cole stood out. While writing this book, I asked a woman I had dated what she remembered about Cole. She told me that, during the first meal we had shared with Cole, she had told Cole that she had Celiac disease and was unable to eat gluten.

She said, "Most teenagers would just think, 'Stinks to be you.' But Cole was so different in so many ways. Weeks later, a book showed up on my doorstep. While having dinner with his mom, Cole had mentioned to her that I was unable to eat gluten. She had a gluten-free cookbook that she never used, and so Cole sent me the book."

It Starts with Self-Respect

Respect starts with respecting ourselves. When we treat ourselves with respect, we avoid self-destructive behaviors and habits. The more respectfully we treat ourselves, the more respectfully we treat others. In turn, others treat us with more respect.

We teach people how to treat us. If we don't respect ourselves, then others won't respect us. People who don't respect themselves allow others to use them and take advantage of them.

In my presentations to high schoolers I try to delicately teach them to be careful about intimacy. If someone's being nice to you only to get something from you, it's not someone you should be with. Respect yourself enough to walk away. Respect yourself enough that you can look back on your life and hold your head up and be proud of your decisions.

"Respect yourself and others will respect you."

—*Confucius*

And don't be that person who only wants to take from others. Healthy relationships are based on trust and respect—what we give to each other, rather than what we take from each other. In all our relationships, our focus should be on what we contribute to the relationship. We give to and serve those whom we respect, and take from those whom we don't respect. And if we find ourselves taking more than we're giving in our relationships, it probably means that we don't respect ourselves enough.

Everyone wants to be respected. The only way we get respect is by giving it. And it starts with giving it to ourselves.

CHAPTER EIGHT

What Matters More than Skills and Stats

"It is your attitude, not your aptitude, that determines your altitude." —*Zig Ziglar*

In the 1998 NFL draft, the Indianapolis Colts had the number one draft pick and an agonizing decision to make. They had to choose between two stellar quarterbacks: Ryan Leaf and Peyton Manning.

Leaf was technically and statistically the more skilled player. His arm strength was almost legendary. He could throw a ball through a car wash and the ball wouldn't get wet. His moves were better, his footwork was better, he just had an unmatched physical presence on the field.

What people said about Peyton Manning was that he was best team player and the hardest worker on the team.

He was very coachable and he made everybody around him better. Still, Leaf was the better player on paper.

Prior to the draft, the NFL holds the Scouting Combine, where college players perform physical and mental tests in front of coaches, general managers, and scouts. The players are also interviewed and go through psychological evaluations. Leaf blew off his interview with the Colts and didn't even show up. In his arrogance about his obvious physical abilities, he didn't think he needed to. He told his agent, "They're good, I'm good."

In contrast, Peyton Manning not only showed up, but he showed up dressed professionally and with a briefcase prepared to take notes. He took notes through the interview and asked a lot of questions. He was respectful and told them, "I'm really looking forward to being a member of the Indianapolis Colts. Thank you in advance for drafting me."

The Colts agonized over the decision and, at the last hour, decided to go with Peyton, based primarily on his attitude and maturity. The San Diego Chargers picked Leaf as the second draft pick. The Colts would not regret their decision. Manning went on to win the Most Valuable Player award in five different seasons, the most of any NFL player ever, whereas Leaf was out of the NFL by 2002 and is considered one of the biggest draft busts in NFL history.

Leaf's career was characterized by poor behavior. He skipped out on mandatory meetings and opted to simply pay the fines. He didn't get along with teammates or the media. He blamed his teammates for his poor play. He developed a reputation for a poor work ethic, many times being found on the golf course while the other quarterbacks were studying film. On one occasion, he lied about a hand injury to get out of practice and played golf instead.

After Leaf's rookie season ended, Charger safety Rodney Harrison described it as "a nightmare you can't even imagine," adding, "If I had to go through another year like that, I'd probably quit playing." When Leaf retired after just four years, Harrison said, "He took the money and ran. Personally, I could never rest good at night knowing my career ended like that. Normally in this game, you get back what you put into it, and he pretty much got back what he put into it."

In May 2009, Leaf was indicted on burglary and controlled-substance charges in Texas. He was fined $20,000 and sentenced to ten years of probation. Three years later, he was arrested multiple times on burglary, theft, and drug charges. In September of 2014, he was sentenced to five years in prison, though he was later released that year.

In contrast, Peyton Manning played eighteen years in the NFL, set many records, including for passing yards and touchdown passes, and is now considered to be one of the greatest quarterbacks of all time.

Consider this staggering career comparison:

Peyton Manning Versus Ryan Leaf

	MANNING	LEAF
Games Started:	265	21
Wins:	186	4

	MANNING	LEAF
Career Passing Yards:	71,940	3,666
Touchdowns:	539	14
Pro Bowl Selections:	14	0
Super Bowl Titles:	2	0

"Ability is what you're capable of doing. Motivation determines what you do. Attitude determines how well you do it." –Lou Holtz

What Stats Don't Show

By all objective standards, Ryan Leaf should have been the better quarterback. He was stronger and faster, he had a better throwing arm, he had better skills, he had better stats. But Peyton Manning had something that mattered far more than all of that: a good attitude. While Leaf was arrogant, Manning was respectful. While Leaf blamed others for his performance, Manning took responsibility. While Leaf slacked, Manning worked his tail off. While Leaf felt entitled, Manning took nothing for granted. When one reporter went to Leaf's hometown to learn more about him, he discovered that no one really liked him. Manning, on the other hand, was just a person that people wanted to be around.

As this contrast vividly shows, attitude is far more important than skills and stats. Take two people with comparable skills, and the person with the better attitude is going to go much further in life, accomplish much more, make a greater difference, and simply enjoy life more. This simple thing called attitude cannot be overestimated! It really is simple, but it is so foundational to a life well lived.

~~~~~~~~~~~~~~~~~~~~~~~~~~~~~

"Talent is cheaper than table salt. What separates the talented individual from the successful one is a lot of hard work."

–Stephen King

~~~~~~~~~~~~~~~~~~~~~~~~~~~~~

It's Not About You

Peyton Manning retired in 2016. After his retirement, he was talked about non-stop for months. He had set so many records, but nobody talked much about that. When his teammates and coaches were interviewed, what they consistently said was, "He made everyone around him better." That was the theme of his career.

Manning reminds me of someone else...yeah, you guessed it. Cole was that kind of person as well, who made everyone around him better. He lifted everyone around him. You were just better for knowing him. As one of his coaches put it, "He would give you the shirt off his back." He was the hardest worker on his team. He was the first to show up and the last to leave. You'd never hear him complain.

Another of his coaches told me a story of when Cole was in 8th grade. He was coaching a summer lacrosse

71

camp designed for kids who just wanted to try out lacrosse to see if they liked it. He said:

> During a couple of the drills, Cole could see that some of the kids were struggling with the basic concepts. Because Cole was already advanced for his age, I asked him to take a few of the boys off to the side and give them some individual attention. I watched Cole work with these young boys as he walked them through, step-by-step, how to execute ground balls and make passes. I was very impressed with his ability to relate to these youngsters and get across to them the fundamentals of lacrosse. He was so willing to set aside his own time to help others.

Kettle Moraine has always had one of the best lacrosse teams in the state of Wisconsin. Every year we're always in the top four, and we won the state D1 championship in 2016 and 2017. I'm not the only one who believes their continued success has been influenced by Cole, even after his death. As one of Cole's coaches and Kettle Moraine's current head coach, Michael Stefan told me, "There is no doubt that Cole's influence still helps guide the program, even for those younger players who have never met him."

Cole was also the most unselfish lacrosse player I've ever seen. In fact, he was a bit *too* unselfish. He played the position of midfielder. It is a position that requires a lot of overall athleticism and a wide range of skills. Middies cover the entire field and are expected to play both offense and defense. Cole was arguably one of the best d-middies (defense) in the Midwest, and definitely in the state of Wisconsin.

As good as he was defensively, offensively he didn't care who scored as long as we scored. In fact, he was just as happy to pass the ball for an assist and let someone else score as he was to take the shot himself. His coaches actually had to get on him a bit for being too unselfish and unwilling to score. He was passing up too many opportunities, and they kept urging him to shoot. He was reluctant because his focus was on making everyone around him shine. To help his team, he had to learn to be more assertive offensively, and he started scoring more his junior and senior years.

"You can easily judge the character of a man by how he treats those who can do nothing for him." *–Malcom S. Forbes*

As people like Peyton Manning and Cole show, having a good attitude means that it's not about you. Living a good life isn't about you and your trophies and awards, your playing time and stats. It's about what you do for other people. It's about how you serve and uplift those around you, and what you do to make others better. It's not about what you can take—it's about what you can give.

PART II

Work Hard and Prepare

The ancient Greek storyteller Aesop is known for his classic fables, including the following story of the grasshopper and the ant.

A good-natured grasshopper spent his days singing. He watched ants working hard to carry food into their home.

The grasshopper said, "Why not come and sing with me instead of working so hard?"

The ants responded, "We're storing food for the winter. You should do the same."

"Winter is far away and it is a glorious day to play," sang the grasshopper.

But the ants went on their way and continued their hard work.

The weather soon turned cold. All the food lying in the field was covered with a thick blanket of snow that even the grasshopper could not dig through. Soon the grasshopper found itself dying of hunger. He staggered to the ants' hill and saw them handing out corn from the stores they had collected in the summer. He begged them for something to eat.

"What?" cried the ants in surprise. "Haven't you stored anything away for the winter? What in the world were you doing all last summer?"

"I didn't have time to store any food," whined the grasshopper. "I was so busy playing music that before I knew it the summer was gone."

The ants shook their heads in disgust, turned their backs on the grasshopper and went on with their work.

As this simple story shows, everybody wants to be successful and prosperous. But surprisingly few are willing to put in the hard work and preparation it requires. In this section, we'll discuss how to lay the foundation of success through preparation and hard work.

CHAPTER 9

Be Proud of Your Work

> "The price of success is hard work, dedication to the job at hand, and the determination that whether we win or lose, we have applied the best of ourselves to the task at hand."
>
> —*Vince Lombardi*

Every time Cole would leave the house, I would tell him the same thing: "Love you, bud. Be proud of your work." He had to have heard that thousands of times in his life—so much that I'm sure he got sick of it.

In fact, one time he *did* get sick of it. His first W-2 job was working for a country club. He would set up tables, fill water glasses, set up banquets, whatever they needed. It was pretty basic, grunt-level work. Still, I taught him to do his best no matter the job. One day, as he was leaving for work, I said it: "Love you, bud. Be proud of your work."

He stopped in his tracks, turned around, and said, "Dad, all I'm doing is filling water. I'm wrapping up utensils. I'm putting napkins on tables and setting out place cards. I'm cleaning tables off."

I didn't miss a beat. I said, "Let me tell you something, son. Country club membership is down. Think of some young lady visiting the club. She's thinking, 'Do I spend $50,000 at this country club for my reception, or should I do it somewhere else?' Or, you could have a prospective member night, where you get prospective members coming in and wondering if they want to join the club or not. If the table settings don't look correct, if the glasses aren't clean, maybe they don't join. Maybe they do something else because they perceive that to be lower quality. What you do is important. Don't ever forget that."

He didn't say a word. He just shook his head and gave me a look like, "I got nothing for that. I'm outta here." But I'm sure he got the lesson.

No Noble Effort is Inconsequential

In our culture, we've come to think that some jobs are more important than others—and therefore, some people are more important than others. We compare ourselves with each other based on how much money we make, how big our house is, how nice our car is. But none of that matters. All that matters is whether or not we put our whole hearts into everything we do.

I'm reminded of a man by the name of Cornelius Washington, a garbage man in New Orleans who was dubbed the "wizard of trash cans." When he died of a heart attack in 2008 at the age of forty-eight, the *New Orleans Times-Picayune* published this tribute for him:

> Washington's street choreography of playful twirling and tossing often prompted applause. With a full trash can in each arm, he would 'pop' both cans upside-down into the truck's metal jaws, then set them back on the curb without losing his stride. From seemingly impossible distances, he would toss dozens of bags and boxes rapid-fire, landing them all in the back of the truck without dropping a scrap of paper.
>
> 'Cornelius was amazing. He could do things that I didn't think that people could do with garbage,' said Dorothy Taylor, who has driven New Orleans garbage trucks for eighteen years. She added, 'He would take one route and do it by himself. He was like two men in one. No machine could beat him. No man could beat him. If he was tired, you'd never know it. He was like a garbage sex symbol.'
>
> ...Washington said hoppers in other cities seemed lackluster. 'It's too textbook,' he said. 'They stop the truck. They step off the truck. They pick up the can. They dump it. Then they put the can back down in that one spot.'
>
> No comparison with New Orleans, where hoppers like him had nearly perfected the art of trash pickup, he said.

'If they was to put a garbage man in the Guinness World Book of Records, I would be in there,' he said.

His boasting wasn't based on showmanship alone. Washington knew where each handicapped and elderly neighbor lived and taught younger hoppers to return cans right to their doors. He also told them to work together with other hoppers on big stacks of refuse and to warn the truck driver about street closings, children, drunks and careless bicyclists.

'Every driver wanted Cornelius on his truck,' Taylor said. 'There will never be another like him.'[10]

We tend to use the belittling "just" when we think of jobs like this. As in, he was "just" a garbage man." Just, nothing. Garbage collecting and disposal is a profound service for humanity. No matter what we're doing we should be proud of our work, and we should put pride into our work. If you're going to do something, then do it with pride.

As Martin Luther King, Jr. said, "If a man is called to be a street sweeper, he should sweep the streets even as Michelangelo painted or Beethoven composed music or Shakespeare wrote poetry. He should sweep streets so well that all the hosts of heaven and earth will pause to say, 'Here lived a great street sweeper who did his job well.'"

Do Things Right the First Time

I mentioned earlier that Cole and I never had a cross word, except for one time when he was in freshman geometry. Business and marketing classes came easy to Cole and he got straight A's. He was average at math, but he really struggled with geometry. We had a tutor for him and that helped. But Cole was slacking a bit.

At one point I said something to Cole about his math grade. He said, "It's okay, dad. I can reassess next Thursday." He hadn't been putting forth his full effort because he was just thinking that he'd get a do-over.

That attitude really rubbed me the wrong way, and I told him so, pretty forcefully. I said, "Dammit, Cole! Don't give me that B.S. about reassessing. Do it right the first time!" Of course, I felt bad afterward and we had a talk about it.

But I wanted to make it clear to him to not think in terms of crutches or do-overs. I wanted to disabuse him of the notion, "I can coast on this test and then reassess." I wanted to teach him to do things right the first time, to give his full effort in everything.

"Success isn't always about greatness. It's about consistency. Consistent hard work leads to success. Greatness will come." —*Dwayne Johnson*

One thing I always teach to youth is, "Why is there always time to do the job over but not to do it right the first time?" We may get do-overs in high school classes, but we don't get them in the important things in life. If we don't spend enough quality time with our children, we don't get a do-over. If we don't prepare and we botch a job interview, they don't call us back for a do-over. If we slack at our jobs and get fired, there's no do-over.

If there's time to do a job a second time, there's time to do it right the first time.

The Little Things Add Up to the Big Things

It could have been a final scene from an inspirational movie. It was the 2016 Division I state championship game. Kettle Moraine was playing against Hudson, a very strong team. We were down four goals with just 2:58 left to play in the game. Our face-off guy was Mateo Salceda, whom Cole had mentored when Mateo was an underclassman. He and the Hudson face-off guy had gone back and forth all game and neither dominated the other.

Our head coach, Michael Stefan, called a time out to regroup. Afterward, they went out onto the field and Mateo focused on just one step at a time. He won one face-off and we took possession and scored. He then proceeded to win three more face-offs in a row, and the team scored on each one to tie up the game with seven seconds left. We ended up winning in overtime to win our first state championship and make school history. It was truly magical.

This is what Mateo said of Cole and this experience:

As I participated on the varsity team my freshman year, there was one person on the team who I always saw as a mentor. That person was Cole. He took me under his wing and taught me so much about lacrosse and life.

One of the biggest lessons I took to heart from Cole was that the little things matter. Whether it was a ground ball, a face-off, or a pass, every little thing added up. He taught me that it doesn't apply only to lacrosse but to life as a whole. That doing the little things in life, and doing them with passion, will lead up to something bigger in life. Such as going to class, doing your homework, and doing everything at 100 percent will always build up to something you want in life.

This is a lesson I think about every day, and I thought about in the state championship game. When my team was down by four goals, I focused on just winning the face-off. By winning one face-off, then winning the ground ball, then getting the possession, only then would I be able to reach the big end result of scoring a goal. That lesson of doing the small things gave me the strength to win the face-offs and help the team make school history.

I will never forget all the things Cole taught me, not only as a lacrosse player, but as a student, and as a young adult.

All too often, we dream about accomplishing big things, but don't do the little day-to-day things required to turn our dreams into reality. When we watch the movie Gandhi, we see a magnificent leader conquering a powerful empire. What we don't see are the lonely years he spent in law school hunched over mind-numbing textbooks in libraries, tediously memorizing case law.

We marvel at Bill Gates' net worth. What we don't see is the years he spent coding seven days a week through all hours of the night in the computer center at the University of Washington. We groove to the Beatles' rock-star albums. But what we've never heard is the music they played in Hamburg, Germany clubs for eight hours a night, seven days a week for years, nor have we seen their hard-earned calluses.

Mateo winning those face-offs was the result of years of prior preparation. And so it is with your life. The great things you accomplish will be the result of the little things you do every day for years that no one will ever see.

Do More Than What You Get Paid to Do

I shared with you how I was on my own at eighteen years old. I was scrambling to survive, taking whatever work I could find. A cousin of mine owned a real estate agency, so I thought I could make a go at that. I attended Sinclair Community College in Dayton, Ohio and got my real estate license. I worked my tail off and had a lot of listings. But this was the tail end of Jimmy Carter's presidency in 1979 and 1980 and prime rate was around 18 or 19 percent. Houses weren't selling and I wasn't making any money.

During that time, I tried my hand at a little side business, a pizzeria restaurant. I made a little money, but not enough to keep doing it.

That was when I stumbled into the dental business. I was working with a head hunter, trying to see what else was out there. All I knew was I wanted to be in professional sales, and to have some recurring income. I interviewed at a few places. One of the interviews was with a dental supply company. Four interviews and a five-hour aptitude test later, I was working for the company selling dental supplies at the ripe age of twenty-one.

Looking back, I wouldn't have hired me if I were them. I was too young, dumb, and arrogant. But thankfully, they kept me. I got through the first couple of years and started to have some success.

I'm fifty-six years old now, and I've had a long and successful career in the dental industry. Not one day goes by that I don't thank the good Lord for guiding me to it. And not a day goes by where I don't try to learn something new to better serve my team, our company, and our customers.

There's a simple philosophy I've always lived by, which has helped me climb in my career: *If you do more than what you're paid to do, sooner or later you will get paid more for what you do.*

I always strive to be underpaid for what I do. Most people think that's strange. Now, don't get me wrong, I want to make as much money as I can. But in whatever position I've been in, I always make sure I'm delivering more value than they're paying me for. That's how you get managers to notice you. That's how you earn more responsibilities. That's how you get promotions and raises. You always want that equity gap.

A good friend of mine, Randy, told me a true story. He lives in Florida now, but he was visiting Michigan, where he's from. At his hotel, he kept noticing a woman who worked there. Every time he saw her, she was hustling and going above and beyond to serve guests. He saw that she worked in a lot of capacities, and she gave her whole heart to everything she was doing. She was so good at what she did that he couldn't help but notice.

This was over a period of several weeks. One day, Randy struck up a conversation with her. He asked her if she was doing what she really wanted to be doing. She said she didn't mind it, but she needed the job and wasn't really making any money at it. He found out how much money she was making, and it wasn't much, especially compared to her effort. She was definitely doing more than what she was getting paid to do.

> **"If a guy pays you five dollars, you give him seven dollars worth of work."** —*Bill Russell*

One of Randy's daughters happened to be a manager for a nursing home and she was looking for a new employee. Randy told her daughter about this woman with the great attitude and strong work ethic. His daughter immediately hired the woman and doubled her income and provided her with benefits. It happened because somebody saw her with a great attitude, working a little harder than what she was paid to do.

When it comes to success, there's no substitute for hard work. In everything we do, no matter how lowly it seems, if we're proud of our work, sooner or later that pride pays off.

"You don't get paid for the hour. You get paid for the value you bring to the hour." *–Jim Rohn*

CHAPTER TEN

Winning Happens Long Before You Hit the Field

"Champions do not become champions when they win the event, but in the hours, weeks, months and years they spend preparing for it. The victorious performance itself is merely the demonstration of their championship character." —*Alan Armstrong*

Jack Nicklaus, widely regarded as the greatest golfer of all time, was once asked about how he practices and prepares for tournaments. He explained, "People think that I'm practicing before I play, but I'm not. I'm just warming up. I practice after I play. The first thing I practice is all the shots I hit poorly that day to get those out of the way. And then I practice all the shots that I didn't have to hit that day. Because if I'm coming down the stretch on Sunday afternoon, and the shot requires a three iron, but I haven't hit a three iron all week, I wouldn't be as comfortable. So I practice after I play."

I should clarify that this was coming from a man whose pre-tournament preparation was legendary. He would typically arrive at a Major tournament location a week before it started in order to practice the course. Whether before playing or after, his preparation was the foundation of his success.

~~~~~~~~~~~~~~~~~~~~~~~~~~~~~~

"Spectacular achievement is always preceded by unspectacular preparation." –*Robert H. Schuller*

~~~~~~~~~~~~~~~~~~~~~~~~~~~~~~

Muhammad Ali, arguably the best boxer who ever lived, had a similar mindset. He was once asked how many sit-ups he could do. He responded, "I don't know. I don't start counting until it starts hurting."

Someone once asked the great minister Dr. Lyman Beecher, "How long did it take you to prepare that sermon?"

He replied, "Forty years."

When asked how long it would take to learn the violin, the virtuoso violinist Felice Giardini replied, "Twelve hours a day for twenty years." And that was coming from a child prodigy on the instrument.

After the great Polish pianist Paderewski played before Queen Victoria, the queen exclaimed, "Mr. Paderewski, you are a genius!"

"Ah, Your Majesty," he said, "perhaps; but before I was a genius I was a drudge."

We all love watching masters in any field perform. We love seeing the public victories. We see who won the major game. But what we don't see is the effort that was put in over years to win that won game. We forget that public victories are preceded by private preparation.

It's the same with all of life. It's easy to look at successful people and think, "They got lucky. It was easy for them." People may get lucky breaks, but luck is preparation meeting opportunity. The harder we work, the luckier we get.

"Chance favors the prepared mind." –*Louis Pasteur*

In his book, *Outliers: The Story of Success*, Malcolm Gladwell provides a fascinating perspective on what it takes to succeed. The most important component is what he calls the "10,000-hour rule," which means that achieving mastery in anything—be it sports, playing an instrument, or computer programming—requires about 10,000 hours of dedicated practice. That translates to about twenty hours a week for ten years.

This rule has emerged in dozens of research studies. As neurologist Daniel Levitin explains,

The emerging picture from such studies is that ten thousand hours of practice is required to achieve the level of mastery associated with being a world-class expert—in anything. In study after study, of composers, basketball players, fiction writers, ice skaters, concert pianists, chess players, master criminals, and what have you, this number comes up again and again…no one has yet found a case in which true world-class expertise was accomplished in less time. It seems that it takes the brain this long to assimilate all that it needs to know to achieve true mastery.

Talent is important. But ultimately, what determines your success isn't your natural talent, but rather what you do with it. As Malcolm Gladwell puts it, "Achievement is talent plus preparation…The closer psychologists look at the careers of the gifted, the smaller the role innate talent seems to play and the bigger the role preparation seems to play."

Our live performances are the product of our prior practice. Winning is the natural result of preparation. We can't expect to hit homeruns if we rarely show up for batting practice.

"The key is not the will to win…everybody has that. It is the will to prepare to win that is important." –*Bobby Knight*

Don't Rely on Rousing Speeches to Win

Everyone loves heart-stirring, blood-pumping halftime speeches in sports movies.

The team is outmatched, whipped, down for the count. Spirits are crushed, heads hang low, tails are tucked between tired legs.

Then, the coach reaches deep into his champion's heart to pull out a rip-roaring speech.

The fog of defeat is pierced by the sun of encouragement. Heads lift and begin to nod, spirits are aroused, and soon the team is shouting their conviction that victory is theirs. Refocused and rejuvenated, they charge the field and win the day.

Halftime emotionalism may make for good Hollywood drama. But true champions *never* depend on it to win. That's according to John Wooden, by far the most successful coach in the history of college basketball. Consider:

- Wooden's UCLA teams won ten NCAA championships in twelve years, including seven in a row.
- He coached eighty-eight consecutive victories, smashing the previous record of sixty.
- His teams enjoyed eight undefeated Pacific conference crowns.
- His unprecedented lifetime winning percentage exceeded 80 percent.

With that context, now ponder his counterintuitive insights into emotion, as revealed in his book, *Wooden: A Lifetime of Observations and Reflections On and Off the Court*:

I believe that for every artificial peak you create, there is a valley. I don't like valleys. Games are lost in valleys. Therefore, I wasn't much for giving speeches to stir up emotions before a game.

If you need emotionalism to make you perform better, then sooner or later you'll be vulnerable, an emotional wreck, and unable to function to your level of ability.

My ideal is an ever-rising graph line that peaks with your final performance. I prefer thorough preparation over some device to make us 'rise to the occasion.' Let others try to rise suddenly to a higher level than they had attained previously. We would have already attained it in our preparation. We would be there to begin with. A speech by me shouldn't be necessary.

If your performance depends on stimulating your emotions at critical moments, something is wrong. It's not sustainable, and neither does it create long-term success. Games are won long before you ever set foot on the court. Larry Bird may have dreamed of holding an NBA championship trophy high under flashing lights. But while he was dreaming, he shot at least 500 free throws every day.

The sugary high of sporadic emotions is nothing compared to the enduring nutrition of preparation. And no amount of positive thinking can compensate for incompetence. So you can dream of glory or think as positively as you want. But when you show up to deliver a speech, close a sale, counsel a wayward youth, perform a surgery, or launch a business, the cold, hard truth is this: Either you're ready or you're not. And no pep talk in the moment, no matter how heartfelt, will change that inescapable fact.

I have the privilege speaking for my company on a regular basis. I'm often asked, "Do you get nervous before you speak?" I am excited before I go on stage, but not nervous. I have already done that speech a hundred times in my head and prepared prior to walking on the stage.

"Give me six hours to chop down a tree and I will spend the first four sharpening the axe."

–Abraham Lincoln

If You Don't Work, Life Doesn't Work

Cole made varsity as a freshman on one of the best lacrosse teams in the state of Wisconsin. He worked hard for his spot and earned it with a lot of blood, sweat, and tears.

Varsity players practice at 6:00 a.m. in March and early April. In Wisconsin, there's barely any light at that time of day and you're breaking up ice on the turf. Then, they'd also have late practices, usually at 8:00 p.m., because they'd let JV practice before them. So a lot of times he'd be getting home at 10:00. He'd take a quick shower, grab a bite to eat, then be up by 5:30 the next morning to do it all over again. His junior and senior years, he was also doing a lot of college prep and AP classes in addition to his normal schedule.

He also earned his spot at Benedictine University through his relentless preparation. Only 6 percent of high school athletes ever play an NCAA sport, and I can promise you that it's the ones who have not just the will to win, but also the will to prepare. Cole was one of those, and I couldn't have been prouder of him.

Cole taught me about hard work and preparation more than I ever taught him. I can't tell you how many times I had the thought, "Am I working as hard as my son? Am I willing to prepare as much as he is?" His work ethic left me with no excuses.

Cole knew, as all winners do, that there are no shortcuts in life. The only place where success comes before work is in the dictionary. Nothing in life works if we aren't willing to work.

Ask anyone if they want to be average, and they'll say, "Of course not." Yet their lack of preparation says otherwise. Everyone wants to win and succeed. But few are willing to prepare. Everyone wants to arrive at the destination, but no one wants to make the trip.

"Hard work beats talent when talent does not work hard." –*Tim Notke*

Going the Extra Mile

We all hate getting stuck in traffic jams. But so many of us are stuck in the traffic jams of life because we do what everyone else does, we go where everyone else goes. We take the "average highway" and find that it's jam-packed with the vast majority of people who settle for average.

There are no traffic jams on the extra mile. Winners do what losers and average people won't. When was the last time you went to practice early or stayed late? When was the last time you showed up for work early or stayed late? When was the last time you went the extra mile in any endeavor? Were you surrounded by people? I'm betting you were all alone.

When it comes to work and career, most people end up just trading time for money. Their attitude is to put in the least amount of effort for the maximum reward. Successful people, in contrast, put in maximum effort and increase their contributions in order to increase their rewards. Most people learn how to do their jobs fairly quickly, then stop learning. I have heard from many people, "I have twenty years of experience." I always wonder, "Is it twenty years of experience, or one year of experience twenty times over?" Successful people don't watch the clock, and they don't see work as just a paycheck. They seek to be a productive member of a team. They work for a greater purpose. They're driven to excel in everything they do.

Successful people win, not because they're more talented or competent, but rather because they're more willing to prepare and work hard behind the scenes.

~~~~~~~~~~~~~~~~~~~~~~~~~~~~~~~~

"I have yet to be in a game where luck was involved. I have yet to be in a game where the most prepared team didn't win." —*Urban Meyer*

~~~~~~~~~~~~~~~~~~~~~~~~~~~~~~~~

CHAPTER ELEVEN

You Become What You Think About

"You are today where your thoughts have brought you; you will be tomorrow where your thoughts take you." —*James Allen*

The word "manifest," defined today as "to make clear or evident to the eye or the understanding," has a fascinating origin. The literal definition of the original word was "caught in the act." The Latin root *manus*, meaning hand, seems symbolic of man using hands for conscious actions, or making choices. Its accompanying root *festus*, meaning "able to be seized or handled," suggest thoughts made real and concrete. In other words, that which is manifested can be felt, touched, realized as tangible.

Thus, to manifest is to reveal your true thoughts, desires, and character through action. It is to be "caught in the act" of who you are. Of course, this applies to both improvement and degeneration. One can be caught in the act of anonymous service, or caught in the act of theft.

No matter where or how you're caught in action, understand that no action can be taken without forming first as a thought. As Plutarch wrote, "An idea is a being incorporeal, which has no subsistence by itself, but gives figure and form unto shapeless matter, and becomes the cause of manifestation." The Proverb states it more succinctly: "As a man thinketh, so is he..."

What we do is a manifestation of what we think. To manifest a better life, you must first envision a better life. In other words, you need a clear, concrete, and compelling vision of your ideal life. Without such a conscious guide, you will manifest the programmed, contradictory, and limiting junk of your subconscious mind. You will be caught in the act of operating on autopilot—blindly accepting social programming, submitting to false labels, believing negative self-talk or the negative talk of others, accepting unquestioningly what is "known" to be impossible.

By default, every human being is a manifester—whether consciously or unconsciously. If you're going to manifest anyway, why not manifest consciously and positively? You must guard your thoughts vigilantly, for they will manifest as either tragic or triumphant actions. As my friend Pete Pulos often says, "Thoughts turn into words, words into actions, actions into habits. And habits determine your destiny and legacy."

Create a Vision of Your Ideal Life

Manifesting what we want is harder than it seems, because so much of our thoughts are subconscious—we're not even aware of them. According to Harvard professor Gerald Zaltman, 95 percent of our thoughts, emotions, and learning occur without our conscious awareness. Most cognitive neuroscientists concur. NeuroFocus founder Dr. A.K. Pradeep estimates it at 99.999 percent.

Dan Ariely, professor of psychology and behavioral economics at Duke University and author of *Predictably Irrational: The Hidden Forces that Shape our Decisions*, concludes from years of empirical research that, "... we are pawns in a game whose forces we largely fail to comprehend."

David Eagleman, neuroscientist at Baylor College of Medicine and author of *Incognito: The Secret Lives of the Brain*, adds that, "...consciousness is the smallest player in the operations of the brain. Our brains run mostly on autopilot, and the conscious mind has little access to the giant and mysterious factory that runs below it."

In his excellent book, *The Ant and the Elephant: Leadership for the Self*, Vince Poscente compares our conscious mind to an ant and our subconscious mind to an elephant. He tells the story of an ant riding on top of an elephant's head. He's trying to get the elephant to get to a certain destination, but the elephant won't listen or take directions. He has to learn how to control the elephant.

So it is with us—our subconscious mind is often running the show. To get our conscious mind in charge, we have to follow these steps, as Poscente details in his book:

1. Clarify your vision.
2. Commit to cultivating positive dominant thoughts.
3. Consistently focus on performance.
4. Strengthen confidence.
5. Control the response to any situation.

Creating your ideal life starts in your mind. What do you want your life to look like? How do you want to spend your time? What do you want your daily life to look like? What types of relationships do you want? How much money do you want to make? What house do you want to live in? Whom do you want to serve? What do you want to contribute to humanity?

Create your vision and write it down. Reflect on it often. The more you do so, the "ant" of your conscious mind will begin guiding the "elephant" of your subconscious mind. As the famous psychiatrist Carl Jung said, "Until you make the unconscious conscious, it will direct your life and you will call it fate."

Your vision is what you hold onto when life gets tough. It's what sees you through the storms of life, as we learn from Florence Chadwick. Florence was the first woman to swim the English Channel in both directions. In 1952 she set out to be the first woman to swim the twenty-one miles from Catalina Island to the coast of California.

The fog was so thick she could hardly see the boats in her own party. Fifteen hours into the swim, she gave up and asked to be pulled out of the water. Her mother and trainer told her she was close and urged not to quit.

When she looked toward the coast, all she could see was the fog. After being pulled into a boat, she discovered that she had been only a half mile from the coast. When the fog shut down her vision, her willpower went with it. Likewise, when we lose our vision, we lose our motivation and willpower and give up. Hold onto your vision!

Focus Your Thoughts by Writing Down Your Goals

Once you have your vision clear, then you want to set clear, measurable goals and write them down.

In 1979 the Harvard MBA program performed a study in which graduate students were asked "Have you set clear, written goals for your future and made plans to accomplish them?"

- 84 percent of students had no goals at all.
- 13 percent had goals but they weren't in writing.
- Only 3 percent had written goals and plans.

Ten years later, the same group was interviewed again and the results were stunning: The 13 percent of the class who had goals, but did not write them down was earning twice the amount of the 84 percent who had no goals. The 3 percent who had written goals were earning, on average, ten times as much as the other 97 percent of the class combined!

All life progress starts with a vision. Once the vision is in place, it must be translated into specific, measurable goals, which answer the critical questions:

1. What are you trying to make happen?
2. How will you measure success?

These goals must be written down, placed prominently, and read out loud daily. A vision without written goals is but a dream. Starry-eyed dreams do come true, but only through wide-eyed, practical plans.

Any successful person I've ever met is great at setting and achieving goals. Only about 3 percent of the dentists I work with have clear, written goals. By far, they are more successful dentists than those who don't write down their goals. And the ones who share their goals with their team are the most successful.

Cole was a great goal-setter and -achiever. For as long as I can remember, he had the goal of getting an MBA. As a freshman in high school, he caught the vision that he could play lacrosse in college, and he focused and worked his butt off to achieve that goal. A great education and career were first in his mind, but he knew that playing a sport in college would be helpful for networking and preparation for a career. If you can play a college sport while getting your degree, it tells employers you're willing to do more than you get paid to do.

Cole's friend, Jake, said of Cole at his funeral, "I always thought [Cole] was just the luckiest kid in the world who could get away with anything. But later on, I realized every action was done for a reason, every word spoken had meaning, and he planned out everything. Whether it was the Rockstar he was getting the next morning, or the hefty investment he was bound to sell six months later, he was always on top of things."

It pains me deeply to think of what Cole could have accomplished had he lived. But I'm grateful that I got to learn from his example while he was alive.

Four People on the Ocean of Life

Author Roy H. Williams writes about the four kinds of people you meet on the ocean of life:

1. Drifters: They just go with the flow. The wind and the waves control their speed and direction. The drifter quietly floats along and says, "Whatever."
2. Surfers: They are always riding a wave, the next big thing. They stay excited until the wave fades away, then they scan the horizon for something new.
3. Drowners: Every time you see them, they're engulfed in one crisis or another. They're always asking to be saved.
4. Sailors: These people are navigating toward a fixed point. They counteract the wind and waves by adjusting the rudder and shifting the sails to stay on course.[11]

Without an immovable, fixed point in your life, there can be no sailing. All you can do is drift, surf, or drown. If you want to sail through life, you must create a clear destination, in the form of vision and written goals. Since you become what you think about, your vision and goals focus your mind on what you want. They are your north star.

Don't just drift through life. Determine what you want, then harness the power of your mind to achieve it.

12

Seize the Opportunity

"Don't wait for extraordinary opportunities.
Seize common occasions and make them great.
Weak men wait for opportunities; strong men
make them." —*Orison Swett Marden*

In lacrosse, the ball is always put into play with what's called a "face-off." Two players from the opposing teams face each other in a crouching position with the ball placed between the two sticks. At a signal from the official, they each try to gain possession of the ball, using their sticks, bodies, and feet. Most times it is a lightning-fast "clamp" and quick possession. Other times, it's like a wrestling match with pads and helmets. Some face-offs can take thirty seconds or longer.

Face-offs are one of the most crucial components of the game, because the more face-offs you win, the more you control the ball. And the more you control the ball, the more opportunities you have to score. Lacrosse is not like football or basketball, where after you score the other team gets the ball back. Good face-off players are therefore worth their weight in gold on the lacrosse field.

Cole had made the varsity team as a freshman, but he didn't see much playing time. The summer between his freshman and sophomore years, his travel team moved him from an attack position to middie. He practiced a ton, they played some great tournaments, and his game really started improving. He also grew a lot.

During football season of his sophomore year, I was at a football game at the high school on a Friday night, standing on the fence line. Cole and I would usually go together, but he'd go hang out with his friends and I wouldn't see him until after the game, then we'd go out to Applebee's. I saw the lacrosse head coach at the time, John, and walked over to him.

I started talking to John. About five minutes later, Cole showed up and stood next to me. I was just telling John, "You're going to see a different kid this year. He's really improved his game. You'll see what he's learned."

John looked at Cole and asked, "What position did you play?"

Cole answered, "They moved me to middie."

John said, "I was going to move you to middie anyway, so that's good."

Then he asked Cole, "Our face-off guy is leaving. Can you take face-offs?"

Cole didn't bat an eye. He immediately responded, "Oh yeah, I can do face-offs."

I was floored—Cole had never taken a face-off in his life! But I tried to hide my shock and affirmed, "Yeah, yeah, he's got face-offs."

We laughed about it afterward. Then Cole went to work to learn face-offs. One of his travel team coaches used to take face-offs in college and knew how to coach them. So Cole took private lessons from him. He took to it really well and never looked back. He loved taking face-offs, and it became a signature part of his game. He became one of the best face-off players in the state, winning close to 80 percent of his face-offs. He was as dominant in face-offs on the east coast as he was in Wisconsin. He became a huge asset to his team by developing this skill.

Preparation, as we've discussed, is vital. But as Cole demonstrated, you have to prepare as much as you can, and then seize those critical moments when they come. Instead of waiting for opportunities, you need to learn how to create your own.

In fact, there's such a thing as over-preparation. People get stuck in "paralysis of analysis" and are too afraid to take action. The whole point of any preparation is to take action—you don't prepare for the sake of preparation alone. If you never take action, all your preparation is for naught.

What's Lost When You Don't Take Action?

Wilson, nicknamed "Woody," was born in 1913 on a small family farm in rural Oklahoma. He and his siblings were not able to attend school regularly, so his mother taught them at home by reading aloud from books she ordered through the mail.

He said, "I thought all books were about 'Little Red Riding Hood' and 'Chicken Little'—girl stories! Then one day Mama brought home a book that changed my life. It was a story about a man and a dog—Jack London's *Call of the Wild*. After we finished reading the book, Mama gave it to me. It was my first real treasure and I carried it with me wherever I went and read it every chance I got."

Through that book, he discovered his dream: He wanted to become a writer and write a boy and dog story. When Woody was sixteen years old, the Great Depression hit and he left home and traveled the country, taking any job he could find. He bounced around for years, working construction jobs in South America, Canada, Alaska.

Along the way, he wrote stories on every scrap of paper he could find. But lacking formal classroom training, his poor spelling and grammar prevented him from selling any manuscripts.

One by one, he locked them away in an old trunk in his father's workshop.

In 1958, he married Sophie Styczinski. Just before their marriage, embarrassed by his failures and committed to being a "responsible" husband, Woody took the old manuscripts from his father's trunk and burned them.

But his dream would not die. Later, he confided his dream to Sophie and told her of the burned manuscripts. She encouraged him to write one of them again. Fighting his insecurities, he rewrote his favorite in three weeks. He handed the rough, unpunctuated manuscript to Sophie and left the house, unable to witness her disappointment. Hours later, he called her to ask her opinion.

"Woody," she said, "this is marvelous. Come home and work on it some more and we'll send it to a publisher."

With her formal education, she helped him polish the manuscript. They ended up selling it to the Saturday Evening Post. The rest is history. That manuscript was *Where the Red Fern Grows*, one of the most beloved stories of all time. To date, almost 7 million copies of the book have been sold.

It's a vivid reminder that we never know what can happen until we try. Wilson Rawls spent years preparing by writing stories. But until he took action to get them published, his preparation did nothing for him—or for the world.

What Can Happen When You *Do* Take Action

In early 1970, a man named Muhammad was a Bangladeshi economist at Chittagong University. After a devastating cyclone, bloody war of independence with Pakistan, and severe famine, Bangladesh was suffering deeply. Muhammad was heartbroken over the poverty he saw, knowing his academic economics were doing nothing to alleviate it.

In 1974 he visited a village to learn directly from the people how to help. He discovered that women creating handcrafts were paying local moneylenders interest rates as high as 10 percent per week. He began loaning these women money from his own pocket, starting with just $27.

From that initial $27 investment, Nobel Prize winner Muhammad Yunus built Grameen Bank, which today has 2,565 branches with 22,124 staff serving 8.35 million borrowers (96 percent women) in 81,379 villages. The microcredit pioneer lends out more than a billion dollars a year in loans averaging less than $200. The bank has lifted millions of illiterate peasants out of the depths of poverty by helping them create small but thriving businesses.

The world is fundamentally, dramatically, and forever changed because one man acted on a prompting to lend twenty-seven bucks to impoverished women making handcrafts. How many times have you received promptings to help others, start a business, make a difference—and not acted on those promptings? What could those ideas have become? Who could they have helped, no matter how insignificant your actions may have seemed in the moment?

Four Questions for Conquering Fear

The reason why we don't act on our opportunities is because we're afraid—afraid of failure, afraid of what people might think of us, afraid of getting hurt, etc. This fear comes from the amygdala, an area in the deepest region of our brain responsible for fear and rage, fight or flight. To watch the amygdala in action, answer these questions based on gut instinct:

- Do more Americans die of suicide or homicide?

- Which is more lethal, kidney disease or AIDS?
- Which is more dangerous: skiing or flying on a commercial aircraft?

Paul Slovic, a psychologist at the University of Oregon, has spent decades studying how we decide what's risky and what isn't. His studies have shown that how risky something actually is has almost nothing to do with how risky we think it is.

For example, most people think skiing is safer than flying on a commercial aircraft, that smoking is less dangerous than being around handguns, that nuclear power plants are riskier than cars.

According to the U.S. government, in the year 2000 nearly twice as many people killed themselves as were murdered, and kidney diseases caused nearly three times as many deaths as AIDS. Although Americans consistently rate nuclear power as one of the most dangerous of all technologies, it's actually safer by any objective measure than most other forms of power. And two of the deadliest things in America are cigarettes and cars. Auto accidents alone kill an average of 115 Americans every day.

What causes such gross distortions in risk analysis and perception is the amygdala.

In contrast to the amygdala, at the front of our brain, just behind our forehead, lies the prefrontal cortex, which is responsible for planning and decision-making. The prefrontal cortex can consciously, judiciously, and accurately analyze risk and perceived threats. It can override the amygdala's fight-or-flight mechanisms. It can guide us to make wiser, better decisions that help us overcome obstacles and reach our goals.

The challenge is that the amygdala is powerful and often locks the prefrontal cortex out of decision-making processes. But there's a formula we can use to help the prefrontal cortex override the amygdala. When we are faced with fear, we can overcome it by answering the following questions:

1. What's the worst possible thing that could happen if my fear occurs?
2. What's the worst possible thing that could happen if I never overcome or eliminate this fear?
3. What's the best possible outcome I can expect if I don't overcome or eliminate my fear?
4. What's the best possible outcome I can expect if I do overcome or eliminate my fear?

Answering these helps us to consciously deal with unconscious, instinctual fear, thus reclaiming our decisions from the amygdala.

I'm sure Cole was a little afraid after he blurted out that he could handle face-offs. But he didn't let a little fear get in his way of seizing an opportunity. There's no shortage of opportunity in the world. There's only a shortage of courage.

PART III

Be a Good Teammate and Friend

A woman known for her good deeds lay on her death bed. She was visited by an angel who told her he would grant her one wish. She said, "Before I die let me visit both hell and heaven."

She was whisked off to a great banquet hall. The tables were piled high with delicious food and drink. Around the tables sat miserable, starving people.

"Why are they like this?" she asked the angel.

"Look at their arms," the angel replied. She looked and saw that attached to the people's arms, just above the elbow, were long spoons. Unable to bend their elbows, the people aimed the spoons at the food and missed every time. Thus, they were hungry, frustrated and miserable.

"Indeed this is hell!" she exclaimed. "Take me away from here!"

She was then whisked off to heaven. Again, she found herself in a great banquet hall with tables piled high. Around the tables sat people laughing, contented, joyful.

"No spoons, I suppose," she said.

"Oh yes, there are," the angel replied. "Look—just as in hell they are long and attached above the elbow. But here, the people have learned to feed one another."

We can't become successful or happy by trying to "feed" ourselves. We need a team to perform at our best and fulfill our greatest accomplishments. In this section, we'll explore what it means to be a good teammate and friend, what the benefits are, and how to be one.

13

CHAPTER THIRTEEN

"You Sit with Me!"

~~~~~~~~~~~~~~~~~~~~~~

"One of the most important things you can do
on this earth is to let people know they are
not alone." —*Shannon L. Alder*

~~~~~~~~~~~~~~~~~~~~~~

Cole's friend, Jake, shared a story about Cole at Cole and Drew's funeral that reveals a lot about how Cole treated people. Here is Jake's story in his own words:

In my early childhood, I usually bounced around with friends. There weren't many that I stayed with for longer than a school year. That is, until I met Cole. Cole and I met on the first day of third grade.

I had moved to my house about two months prior, leaving me a nervous wreck about being alone with no friends on a brand new bus route. I took my first step on to see an entire bus full of kids I had never seen before. All I could do was stand there frozen.

Then I heard a voice call out my name. I looked over and there I saw a kid with a buzz cut and a big smile on his face. He said, 'You sit with me!' as excited as could be. I had no idea who this kid was, but he greeted me like an old friend. We instantly clicked. We talked the whole ride and hated that we had to part ways once we arrived at our different classrooms.

The next day, I forgot his name. But it didn't matter. He didn't hate me or get mad. He just laughed with that big grin, told me again, and the conversation continued. From then on, Cole Philhower was my best friend. I had never met anyone like Cole. I could tell him anything without having the fear of him going and telling anybody. He was a true friend. The more time I spent with him, the more I grew to love him. With every sport we played together and every trip we took together, the more we got to know each other, the more I knew him as my brother...

Cole was an amazing friend. He would always be there for you when you needed to get out of the house. All he needed was a call and ten minutes later, the Jeep would roll up the driveway, music blaring, and off you went. It didn't matter that he got twelve miles to the gallon on a good day. His friends were more important. Need a ride to practice? Need a ride to school? Cole was more than happy to pick you up and never asked for anything in return.

Over the ten years that I knew Cole, we never had a rough go at our friendship. There was never drama, only good memories...

In that simple story, I find a profound truth about friendship: Be the one who says, "You sit with me!"

Everyone Needs a Friend

Life is hard, and everyone we meet every day is struggling in some way or another. Just as Jake tried to hide his fear about being the new kid at school, these struggles are almost always private. We don't open ourselves to vulnerability because we're afraid of feeling weak, afraid that people won't understand. Yet we're all struggling.

In our struggles and pain, we all need someone to tell us, "You sit with me!" We need someone who will reach out to us and open their arms and hearts in kindness and compassion. It's one of the most comforting and healing things we can ever experience.

Author Melody Ross posted an article online in 2015, entitled "We Must See Past What It Seems...," which went viral. After detailing a heart-wrenching personal story, she says she wishes she could have worn a sign around her neck during that time that said, "My life is falling apart" so that others could have been more compassionate.

Then, she writes, "WHAT IF we could all wear a sign that said what WE REALLY MEANT? What if we could go straight past the small talk……or the masks……and we could actually go straight to the heart of the matter…… what if our friends and family wore signs like this:

- 'My mother can't remember me.'
- 'We are losing our beloved home.'
- 'I just found out my child has cancer, and it's bad.'
- 'I'm going through a painful divorce.'

If we could see those signs, she concludes, "…we would treat each other differently."[12]

The thing about Cole is that he didn't need to see a sign on someone. If you were a human being, that's all he needed to be your friend. He was the guy that everyone felt like they could sit with or go to whenever they needed help or comfort.

Everyone Wants to Feel Included

Dylan Patscott was another of Cole's close friends. He shared with me another story about the kind of friend Cole was, from which we can all learn.

He said,

I first met Cole when I moved schools in fifth grade. At that time, I was really shy and quiet. I really kept to myself. Cole and I were in the same homeroom for math and English. My desk was in the back, right by the teacher. It was a real quiet area over by the window. I would usually spend most of my time staring out the window waiting to go home.

There was this kid up front who would always talk and interrupt class. It honestly annoyed me. I thought, 'Man, this kid just does not shut up.' My desk sat next to an empty desk. And I always feared that if this kid didn't stop talking, he'd get moved back to that empty desk beside me. And then he would talk all the time and I would have no idea what to do.

Sure enough, about halfway through the year, Cole was talking again and the teacher told him, 'You need to move back by Dylan.' I thought, *Oh, no. It's coming true. This is my nightmare day.*

Cole stood up, turned around, and said, 'Alright, Dylan, where you at?' I raised my hand sheepishly. He said, 'I'm coming back by you, bro.' He sat down by me and the very first thing he said was, 'You don't talk very much, do you?'

I said, 'Not really.'

He responded, 'Oh, that's okay. Talking is overrated.'

I thought, 'That's weird. All you do is talk.'

From then on, he and I sat together. Over time, I started opening up. He was the light of the class. Everyone knew him and he talked to everybody. He was like a Walmart greeter. And he started introducing me to all his friends. This opened the door for me to make my own friendships. He really made me feel included.

Looking back, it's weird because he was the kid I dreaded to sit next to. But he ended up being one of the best friends I've ever had. He went from a person who I didn't even want to meet to a person who I've tried to emulate.

Cole could win anyone over because he was so inclusive and caring. He was never too good for anyone. There was no one he couldn't bond with. He looked past all differences. He didn't see "jocks," "nerds," "preppies," or "stoners." He didn't see "popular" or "unpopular." He didn't see "pretty" or "ugly." All he ever saw were people. And that was good enough for him. As Dylan said of him, "When we were at Cole and Drew's funeral, I've never seen more people call one person their best friend."

At Cole's funeral, one of his coaches, Jerod, said, "Cole wasn't about who you are or where you came from. He was taught to show everyone respect and love, and that's how he lived his life. He didn't care what your past was like or what you did wrong that day. As long as you showed him and the others around him respect, he would do the same."

Courtney was a girl Cole dated seriously for about a year and a half until the accident. I asked her to share with me some things she remembered about Cole. She talked about how when Cole would hang out at her house, she just wanted him to herself. But Cole would always sit down in the family room and start talking to her family. She said, "I didn't want to talk to my boring family. But he was so interested in talking to my mom or my brother about whatever had happened that day." Her little brother was three years younger than Courtney, and he was a freshman when Cole and Courtney were seniors. Courtney told me how impressed her brother was that Cole was so friendly to him, both at her house and at school. The age and grade difference didn't matter to Cole.

~~~~~~~~~~~~~~~~~~~~~~~~~~

"Service is the rent we pay for living. It is the very purpose of life and not something you do in your spare time." –*Marian Wright Edelman*

~~~~~~~~~~~~~~~~~~~~~~~~~~

Courtney also shared with me how, when she and Cole were dating, there was a disabled girl at the school who had a crush on Cole and flirted with him a lot. Courtney said, "Every time that she would get around Cole she would get really nervous and start to blush and stutter. And he would always stop and talk with her and make her feel very welcome. She would comment on his photos and everything on Facebook, and he would make really sweet comments back. He never demeaned her and just always made her feel special."

Another of Cole's friends, Peyton, shared with me his memory of his first time hanging out with Cole. He was a sophomore and couldn't drive, and Cole was a junior and had his license and a car. They were allowed to drive off-campus for lunch, but Peyton was stuck at the school. He said, "Cole offered to take me and a couple buddies who couldn't drive out for lunch. And we had a great time. He did stuff like that quite a few times, just helping out people who couldn't do things. He cared about his friends and would be there to help anyone who needed it."

What a world this would be if we could all take lessons on friendship from Cole. If we all had people like Cole in our lives, we'd feel so much more safe, comfortable, and valued. We'd be so much more open and real with each other. We'd all feel so much better about ourselves. Knowing there was someone who saw the best in us, we'd all strive to live up to that.

Unfortunately, not everyone we interact with is like Cole—in fact, very few people are. We can't control how others treat us. The only thing we can control is how we treat others. The best we can do is be the kind of person who sees people in their struggles and says, without hesitation, "You sit with me!"

"If you are nice to me, I will be nice to you."

-Max Pulos

14

Stand Up When It Matters

~~~~~~~~~~~~~~~~~~~~~~~~~~~~~~~~

"Stand up for what is right, even if you're
standing alone." —*Suzy Kassem*

~~~~~~~~~~~~~~~~~~~~~~~~~~~~~~~~

Given the choice, Kitty Genovese would rather not have become the subject of social psychology research.

As she was returning home from work on March 13, 1964, Kitty was approached by a man who attacked and stabbed her. She screamed repeatedly for help. At least a dozen people heard her screams, but it took a full thirty minutes before someone contacted the police.

Four years later, researchers John Darley and Bibb Latane, fascinated by the Kitty Genovese case, first demonstrated the "bystander effect" in the lab. The greater the number of people present, they discovered, the less likely people are to help a person in distress.

For example, they staged an experiment around a woman in distress. 70 percent of the people alone called out or went to help the woman after they believed she had fallen and was hurt. But when there were other people in the room only 40 percent offered help.

The bystander effect is explained by what social psychologists call "diffusion of responsibility": In a large group of people, people may feel that individual responsibility to intervene is lessened because it is shared by all of the onlookers.

The bottom line is this: People tend to follow the crowd and cave to social pressure. We tend to drown out the voice of conscience when people around us are taking a different path than us.

Be the One People Can Count On to Be There for Them

From a young age, Cole was always one to stand up against abuse and injustice, and I always admired that about him. When he was in second grade, one of the boys in his class threatened to poke a girl with a sharp pencil. Cole stepped in between them and intervened. Later, we received a call from the girl's mother. She wanted to thank Cole for being so thoughtful and upstanding.

Cole wasn't a big fighter. His style was to talk himself out of situations. Or he'd say some smart aleck remark to make people feel foolish. He wasn't malicious at all. He was clever and quick on his feet. But if he saw someone else getting picked on, or especially if he saw someone mess with one of his friends, he was instantly there to get their back. If you had a problem with any of Cole's friends, you had a problem with Cole.

Cole's senior year, his team played one of their rivals, Lakeshore. Every game they played against Lakeshore was "chippy" and heated, and this game was no exception. The friction started in warm-ups before the game had even begun. During the game one of our players, Mike, got hit hard with a cheap shot that knocked him to the ground. The Lakeshore player who hit Mike was the coach's son. He was a big kid, and their star player. This all happened right in front of the other team's coaches.

Cole wasn't close to all of this when it happened. But when he saw the Lakeshore player knock Mike down, he bolted and ran right into the middle of the fight. He didn't slow down or stop—he ran straight into the kid and drilled and buried him. He went down hard, right in front of his dad, the coach. His dad threw off his coaching hat, ran out onto the field, and grabbed Cole, which is virtually unheard of. (As you can imagine, I wasn't too happy about it at all, and I had words with the coach after the game.)

By this time, both teams were out on the field. Cole pulled off his chin strap from his helmet, which could have easily got him rejected. (That's a really big deal in the sport.) He was pointing and yelling at the coach, "Keep your hands off of me! You can't do that!"

It eventually settled down. But it just showed Cole's nature. He would never pick a fight. If someone had a personal problem with him, he'd avoid it. But he had a huge loyalty streak for his friends. As his friend and coach, Jerod, said of this situation, "As soon as someone stepped on his friend's toes he'd be the first one there for support. He proved that to everyone in the game versus Lakeshore. After a late hit on a fellow teammate, after the play, Cole was the first one there to knock the kid to the ground. Like an enforcer does in hockey, Philhower rallied his team back from a four-goal deficit to beat Lakeshore 6 to 5."

Furthermore, Cole had a broad definition of "friend." Pretty much, if you knew Cole, he considered you to be his friend. And he treated all his friends equally. As one of his friends, Luc, told me,

> He had so many friend groups he would just be constantly bouncing around. He hung out with so many different people. But you always felt like Cole would be there for you as much as he would be any other friend. And you'd never feel like anyone else was taking priority. He brought all his friends together. Cole would never make you feel like he was ditching you or choosing someone else over you.
>
> After he passed, I was amazed to see how many people came together who were part of his inner circle. We all wanted to honor Cole one more time and say, 'Hey, we were all part of this close group who all felt Cole made us feel special.' He was so genuine, and he was able to be genuine with everyone and make everyone feel like they were getting him 100 percent. I think that's really special.

Stand Up and Be Counted

During Stalin's rule of the Soviet Union in the 1950s, Nikita Khruschchev was the leader of the Communist Party. After Stalin's death, Khrushchev visited the United States and gave a press conference.

He was given a written question from a reporter, "Today you talked about the hideous rule of your predecessor, Stalin. You were one of his closest aides and colleagues during those years. What were you doing all that time?"

Khrushchev glared at the audience, his face reddening in anger. "Who asked that?" he roared.

Silence from the audience.

Once again he bellowed, "Who asked that?"

Dead silence.

After a long pause, Khrushchev said quietly, "That's what I was doing."

A few years earlier, a Protestant pastor in Germany named Martin Niemoller was released from a Nazi concentration camp after seven years of imprisonment and wrote:

> First they came for the Socialists, and I did not
> speak out
> Because I was not a Socialist.
> Then they came for the Trade Unionists, and I did
> not speak out
> Because I was not a Trade Unionist.
> Then they came for the Jews, and I did not speak out
> Because I was not a Jew.

Then they came for me—and there was no one left to speak for me.

The daily challenges you and I face aren't anywhere close to standing up against a Holocaust. But that's kind of the point. If we're not willing to stand up for the little things, will we be willing to stand up for the big things?

~~~~~~~~~~~~~~~~~~~~~~~~~~~~~~~~~~~~~

"All that is necessary for the triumph of evil is that good men do nothing." *–Edmund Burke*

~~~~~~~~~~~~~~~~~~~~~~~~~~~~~~~~~~~~~

All of us have opportunities to stand up against abuse and injustice. To speak up and speak out. To stand up and protect our friends. We certainly don't have to be social justice warriors running around and constantly wailing about everything wrong with our society. But like Cole standing up for that girl in second grade, we can quietly make our presence felt in meaningful ways. As Albert Einstein said, "The world is a dangerous place, not because of those who do evil, but because of those who look on and do nothing."

Don't be a bystander on the sidelines of life. Don't be a casual onlooker when you see people struggling or being bullied. Take responsibility. Step up and step into situations and do what you can to make a difference. For as Martin Luther King, Jr. said, "The ultimate measure of a man is not where he stands in moments of comfort and convenience, but where he stands at times of challenge and controversy."

15

You Can't Accomplish Anything as a Lone Wolf

"Alone we can do so little, together we can do so much." —*Helen Keller*

One of the things Cole constantly heard from me was, "Everything you ever want to get done in life, you have to get done through other people." There are very few professions or organizations where you can simply be a lone wolf and be successful. It's virtually impossible. I suppose a person could be the best neurosurgeon in the world and not connect with other people and still make a great living. But for the vast majority of people, learning how to cooperate with others is one of the most important skills we can learn.

Your ability to get along with other people is one of the most powerful assets you'll ever possess. I'm sure you've heard the term, "It's not what you know, it's who you know." That's true, to a certain extent. But if you can't get along with people, it doesn't matter who you know. You could know a ton of highly successful people, but if they won't take your phone call because of how you treat people, what good does it do for you?

Your ability to rise is only equal to your ability to help other people rise. The better you treat people and cooperate with them, the more you'll be able to accomplish.

There's No "I" in "Team"

Yes, I know it's a cliché and you've heard it a thousand times. But it really is true, and it's critical to understand. Selfish people may have great personal stats. They may get a lot of accolades. But ultimately, if you want to win anything of real importance, you have to do it as part of a team.

Cole's friend, Luc, explained to me how Cole exemplified this principle. Luc's family had moved to Australia, where he really struggled with making friends. When they moved back to the States, he was really hoping he could make friends here. He started playing lacrosse at Kettle Moraine when he was a junior and Cole was a sophomore. He was a great player. He and Cole met in a summer lacrosse league. He said he was immediately drawn to Cole because of his maturity, his commitment to the sport, and, most importantly, his ability to be a team player.

He told me:

When he was on the field, he didn't care about any differences between you. He didn't care how he felt about you or if he didn't know you. If you were on his team, he treated you just like he treated any other teammate.

When we started playing together, I hadn't played for a while and I was really rusty. Cole didn't know me but he took so many opportunities to get me into the game, pass me the ball, and set up shots for me. Right away, I could tell this guy was such a team player, and I hit it off with him.

The classic situation with talented high school players is that they take the ball and run it themselves. They're not team players. They're selfish. They don't respect other players, and they don't give other players equal opportunity. Although Cole was one of the most talented players on the field, he was never this way. He was such a selfless player. If a pass needed to be made, he would do it, regardless of who he was passing to. He would never just try to run it through an impossible wall of defense.

He also would never beat people up for mistakes. Rather, he was super encouraging. He knew that everyone makes mistakes and everyone is developing. He was very patient and helpful with other players.

One of Cole's coaches, Al, added, "One thing that really sticks out in my mind about Cole is that he was so respectful. He'd give you the shirt off his back. He gelled with many of the kids, not only on the lacrosse field, but the school as well. When Cole was a senior, one of my other boys made varsity as a freshman. And this younger kid was leery because he didn't know a lot of the older players. Cole took him and some of the other younger boys under his wing and was such a great leader, teacher, and role model."

Another of his coaches, Michael Stefan, said simply, "Cole was mature enough to see the greater picture and what was important, not just concerned about himself or his wants and needs."

Every great team needs great individual players. But the better those individual players can work together, the more everyone can accomplish together. Selfish players may win scoring titles, but selfless team players win championships.

Consciously Cultivate Relationships

I really wish I would have understood the value of networking at a young age. It's a skill I've had to learn. Remember: Everything you want to accomplish must be done with and through other people. The more people you know and have genuine relationships with, the higher and faster you can rise and the more you can accomplish.

A quick story on this. Remember the story of when I told Cole I wanted to speak in high schools to students? After Cole's death, I decided to pursue it, starting with Kettle Moraine High School. Obviously, a person doesn't just walk off the street and start speaking at a high school assembly. I had to find an avenue to get it done.

I mentioned it to some of my close friends, Curt and Traci. Curt said that I could probably speak at a "Life of an Athlete" event, which was a standard thing at our high school where different speakers would come in and talk to the kids. Curt and Traci knew Mike Fink, the athletic director for our school. They mentioned my thoughts to Mike and told him I do a bit of public speaking for my company and that I might have a good message for the kids. Mike and I had met over the years but we didn't really know each other well at the time. Mike listened, then took it to the school administrators. Eventually, I was asked to speak. But if Mike hadn't respected my friends who mentioned me, it never would have happened. That's not a huge deal, but it shows how it works: If we want something, we have to work with other people to get it.

If I'm hiring someone, all things being equal, I'll lean towards the person who comes highly recommended from someone I trust. But no one wants to get burned because he or she hired the wrong person—someone with a poor attitude, a poor work ethic, or no desire or ability to be a team player. So the more people who know and trust you, the more likely you are to get opportunities.

Here are five ways to strategically cultivate relationships to boost your opportunities:

1. Be Genuinely Interested in Other People

When you're in social settings, don't talk about yourself. Ask questions of other people, then sit and listen. Find out what's important to them, what jazzes them, how they see the world. When they're talking, don't look around the room. Focus intently on them and what they're saying. Make them feel like they're the only person in the room.

I look at everyone as if they have a sign on their head that says, "Make me feel important." People won't always remember what you said but they always remember how you made them feel. People come alive when others show genuine interest in them. If you do that, they'll always remember you.

2. Simple Politeness Goes a Long Way

Always say "please" and "thank you." Look for opportunities to serve. Make it a habit to send thank-you notes to people when they host events or do nice things for you. It's a simple thing, but it really stands out, especially in the digital media age, when handwritten notes are so rare.

3. Focus on What You Can Give, Not What You Can Get

Don't go into networking scenarios thinking of what you're trying to gain. Focus instead on listening to people to learn how you can create value for them. People are not impressed by your accomplishments—they're impressed by the attention you give to *them*.

4. Follow Up and Follow Through

You'd be surprised by how far a little follow-through can take you. Very few people really follow through on commitments, so if you do it, you'll stand out. Be the one people can count on to follow through on your commitments. When you meet people for the first time, look for things you can do for them, then follow up later and actually do them. Don't be the person who takes a business card and is never heard from again.

5. Keep it Real

Facebook and LinkedIn can be a good way to stay connected, but that's not networking. Meet people face to face. Look them in the eyes. Create real human relationships. In our digital age, this is more important than ever.

Your ability to succeed in life is largely determined by your ability to work well and get along with others. As an old African proverb puts it, "If you want to go fast, go alone. If you want to go far, go together."

16

You Can't Do It Alone

"God doesn't intend for you to handle all the pain and stress in your life by yourself. We were wired for each other. We need each other."

—*Rick Warren*

I was raised Catholic and attended a Catholic grade school. Every day I wore black pants, a white shirt, and a black clip-on tie. I was an altar boy as well. Truth be told, we were more "holiday Catholics"—we attended mass on Christmas Eve, Easter, and maybe a few special events.

Cole was raised in a similar fashion. He was baptized Catholic and, though he went to public schools, his mother involved him in Sunday School and church activities. But we really were not that much better at going to church than how I grew up.

Drew's family are devout Christians and very involved with a local non-denominational congregation called Elmbrook Lake Country Church. Many times, when Cole would sleep over on a Saturday at Drew's house, I would get a text on Sunday morning saying, "Hey Dad, I am going to church with Drew. I will be home after." He would often see his coaches or teachers at church.

As a parent, one of the many things you never think about is what type of funeral service you would have if your child passed away. We were members of St. Anthony Church. I wondered if we should have Cole's service there. But we decided to have a joint service with Cole and Drew at Elmbrook. It's a good-sized church that seats 1,200. Extra seating was brought in to make it 1,500. The two receiving lines were filled for hours prior to the service. There was standing-room only in the back of the church. It is impossible to know how many attended the service, including the folks who came through the receiving lines but could not stay for the service. It was easily thousands.

Three weeks after Cole's service, I was drawn to Elmbrook. I just felt I needed to attend the upcoming Sunday service. I saw John and Nancy (Drew's parents) as I was walking in, and we sat together. Since that day, I have attended services every Sunday that I am in town, which is most Sundays. I suppose seeing John and Nancy that morning was destiny, as we do not always see each other at the beginning of services.

Elmbrook has been such a great source of support for me. Everyone has been so kind to me. So many people came up and introduced themselves to me during that initial period after the funeral. As you can imagine, one's faith is quite tested when a tragedy like this happens. You think, "How could God let this happen? How could you take two of the greatest kids we will ever know from us?"

Although it was an incredible challenge in the beginning, my faith has grown in these past few years. Obviously, there are no answers, just the questions. But I continue to try to be a better believer, to be a person of faith, to try to see how this tragedy somehow fits into God's plan. As my friend Pastor Scott Grabendike said to me, "Puzzles can be solved. Mysteries we have to live with."

What I know for certain is this: We need to rely on other people for support during tragedies and hard times. Just as our accomplishments must happen with and through other people, so must our grieving. The more we try to bear our burdens by ourselves, the more we suffer. Conversely, the more we open our hearts and allow others to help us bear our burdens, the lighter they become.

I'll be forever grateful to everyone in my life who has been there for me during this tragedy. And I hope I can be there for others as well.

The Core Human Need

Underneath all our differences in worldview, personality, and opinion are universal human traits and needs. We all laugh, we all cry. We all want to be happy and at peace. We all want to feel like we belong and that we matter. We all want meaning in our lives. We all care about family and friends. Underneath all the things that drive us apart, we're really not that different.

What every human being wants, more than anything else, is connection. Brené Brown is a world-renowned researcher who has spent over a decade studying vulnerability, courage, worthiness, and shame, and has published her findings in four bestselling books. In her book, *The Gifts of Imperfection*, she defines connection as "the energy that exists between people when they feel seen, heard, and valued; when they can give and receive without judgment, and when they derive sustenance and strength from the relationship."

This is why seeking support during difficult times is so vital: Connection is the thing that gets us through them. Without connection, our troubles are compounded. With connection, they are alleviated.

Why Connection is Difficult and Scary

Opening our hearts and seeking help with alleviating our burdens and meeting our needs can be a scary proposition. Seeking support and communicating our needs makes us feel vulnerable. Vulnerability feels weak. And weakness feels scary. It feels like we're exposing a soft spot. We don't want to set ourselves up for failure— if we communicate our needs to someone and he or she doesn't respond, where does that leave us? Feeling more weak, vulnerable, and uncared for than before. We also fear that if we expose our soft spot, people will take advantage of us or share our secrets with others.

What we often do instead of opening ourselves up to vulnerability is shield ourselves by being closed, defensive, cynical. As Buddhist teacher Pema Chödrön explains in her book, *The Wisdom of No Escape*, "We all have a soft spot and negativity and resentment and all those things occur because we're trying to cover over our soft spot...it's because you are tender and deeply touched that you do all this shielding. It's because you're soft and have some kind of warm heart, an open quality, to begin with that you even start the shielding."

Open Your Heart to Find the Connection You Seek

Our shield of defensiveness and criticism appears to protect us, but actually prevents us from getting our needs met—particularly the need of connection. *The "soft spot" is where deep connection is found. If we can't access and share our soft spot through vulnerability, we have no hope for real connection.*

In her phenomenal book on vulnerability, *Daring Greatly*, Brené Brown explains the difference between vulnerability and weakness:

> According to the Merriam-Webster Dictionary, the word vulnerability is derived from the Latin word *vulnerare*, meaning 'to wound.' The definition includes 'capable of being wounded' and 'open to attack or damage.'
>
> Merriam-Webster defines weakness as the inability to withstand attack or wounding. Just from a linguistic perspective, it's clear that these are very different concepts, and in fact, one could argue that weakness often stems from a lack of vulnerability—when we don't acknowledge how

and where we're tender, we're more at risk of being hurt.

The less vulnerable we allow ourselves to be in relationships, the greater chance we have of getting hurt. Conversely, the more vulnerable we are, the greater likelihood we have of getting our needs met and feeling connection. The truth is that we find our strength in vulnerability. As we open our hearts to others, we gain the strength we need to carry our burdens. This was so hard for me to learn. Prior to Cole's accident, I was definitely an emotional "lone wolf."

I will be forever grateful for the many get-togethers my friend Traci organized, and the friends who came. I'm so thankful for my many co-workers who were and are still there for me in so many ways. What I did not realize until long into my process was that all of these friends were grieving too! We have to open up and let others step into our pain.

Don't try to bear your suffering alone. It's not enough for us to be a good friend to other people. We must also let others be good friends to us. This means opening our hearts and our lives to connection, especially in our darkest moments when it can be tempting to try to retreat into ourselves. Healing cannot take place in isolation.

17

Am I that Good of a Friend?

"A real friend is one who walks in when the rest of the world walks out." –*Walter Winchell*

On Friday evening, the day of the accident, a lot of people showed up at my house. A friend of mine noticed several of Cole's friends crying in his bedroom. She asked me, "What do you think about having an open house?"

I said, "That's a good idea."

The next morning, I got up and sent out just two text messages—one to one of Cole's friends, and another to one of my adult friends. That's all I did. The day after that, on Sunday, over 300 people showed up at my house. Jimmy John's, where Cole had worked, sent three deliveries at no charge, each one of which fed ninety people. That food was all gone and a lot of people didn't even eat, plus others had brought food themselves.

I also mentioned in the last chapter that thousands of people showed up for Cole and Drew's funeral. I was blown away by that overwhelming outpouring of love and support.

At the funeral, a friend asked me, "How are you even standing?"

I responded, "Cole's holding me up." But in truth, thousands of people were holding me up. My close friends were holding me up. My family was holding me up. Cole's friends, teammates, and coaches were holding me up. My work friends and colleagues were holding me up. People whom I didn't even know from the community showed up to hold me up.

I can't begin to recount the many, many kindnesses that have been extended to me. The support I have received has been unbelievable, from business friends from all over the country, close friends and co-workers who have become family, and friends who have become close friends. Acquaintances and people I used to just nod at and say "hello" to have been there for me, even if it was just with an understanding smile. So many people whom I had never met prior to the accident have stepped up to help in some way. So many people showed up with meals, helped with making funeral and other arrangements, or just offered their condolences. Several of Cole's friends and their parents, Kevin and Curt, worked so hard to put together a tribute video for the funeral. I was so numb for much of the time following the accident that I'm certain I don't remember half of what was done for me.

So many friends of mine and Cole have worn Cole's memorial wristband for years. So many friends have helped with fundraisers. People who I don't even know are supporting me, Cole's memory, and his foundation in so many ways. It is unbelievably humbling for me. All that we have accomplished and will continue to accomplish for Cole would not be possible without this support.

I suppose these people were there all along in my life. But my life was literally Cole and my career, in that order. A tragedy can bring people and communities together, but that usually wanes. As of the writing of this book, it has been three years since the accident. The support is still there, and I experience it daily.

"The friend in my adversity I shall always cherish most. I can better trust those who helped to relieve the gloom of my dark hours than those who are so ready to enjoy with me the sunshine of my prosperity." –*Ulysses S. Grant*

Through all this time, as I watched people give so freely of themselves and their time, I often had the thought, "Would I be that good of a friend?" To this day that question really presses on me. I've wondered how often I have missed out on opportunities to reach out and uplift others. I've wondered how many times I've not been sensitive enough to notice other people in their struggles. That's one of the tender mercies I've seen after losing Cole—the love of family, friends, and other people being revealed to me so clearly and abundantly.

Be Sensitive to the Needs of Others

Cole and Drew's accident was such a big deal that people couldn't help but hear about it, even if they didn't know them. For weeks, high school classmates, teammates, parents of students, and friends held vigils at the site of the accident. The community was in shock. It was a highly-publicized tragedy that brought the community together.

But if you look around, you'll find that everyone is struggling with their own private tragedies, which very few, if any, people know about. And more often than not, we don't pick up on those because we're so engrossed in our own battles and struggles. It takes a conscious effort to pull our heads out of our own struggles and notice those of others. God knows how hard it is for me to pull myself out of my grief to be with others in theirs. But it's worth the effort.

It starts with understanding that no one is immune to misfortune. Life is hard, and *everyone* is fighting one private battle or another. Even the people who appear to have it all together are struggling with things, many of which we can't begin to imagine. As we move through life, we must always just assume that everyone we meet is suffering. Everyone we meet could use a kind word, an uplifting hand.

Next, understand that no one wants or needs us to "fix" anything for us. More precisely, most struggles simply *can't* be fixed, so trying to fix them is meaningless.

All people really want is to know that you're there for them in their struggles, that you feel and empathize with their pain.

What people want isn't pity or advice. What they want is compassion. The word *passion* means "to suffer." The prefix *com* means "with." Compassion, therefore, means "to suffer with."

It means seeing people in their suffering, and just being with the suffering, without trying to change or fix it. It's just holding people in a warm and open-hearted embrace, feeling the suffering, grieving for it, supporting people in it.

"Sometimes our light goes out, but is blown again into instant flame by an encounter with another human being." –*Albert Schweitzer*

As author Parker J. Palmer said, "Here's the deal. The human soul doesn't want to be advised or fixed or saved. It simply wants to be witnessed—to be seen, heard and companioned exactly as it is. When we make that kind of deep bow to the soul of a suffering person, our respect reinforces the soul's healing resources, the only resources that can help the sufferer make it through."

Things to Avoid Saying When Trying to Comfort People

After Cole's death, I had so many people say so many things to try to comfort me with encouraging platitudes. In all honesty, very little of it helped—in fact, many times it would actually make me irritated. I know that their hearts were in the right place and that they simply didn't know what to say. I certainly don't blame anyone for anything that was said. Had I not experienced what I have, they are things that I might have said myself. But after going through what I've gone through, I have a new sensitivity to words of comfort, and I see things differently.

For example, one common thing I heard was, "Cole is in a better place."

Every time I heard it I would think, "A better place? *Really*?! What was wrong about our life?" Of course, nothing is perfect, but it was perfect for us! Cole had a beautiful life growing up. He had an all-American high school and youth experience. He worried for nothing. Relationships came easy for him. He was the best son a man could ask for, and I can't imagine any father and son having a better relationship than we had.

I challenge the people who say this to pick one of their children whom they would choose to be in a "better place." Even if it's true, it's just not a particularly comforting thing to say to those who have just lost a child.

Another thing I heard a lot was, "Well, you'll always be his dad."

I would think, "Do you see him? Look around! Do you see him? Is he here? Did you see him somewhere I didn't see him? Let me go do some parenting with him now!"

Other people have told me, "You have his memory."

Can I give that memory a hug? Can I have a conversation with that memory? Can I watch that memory play lacrosse today, or watch that memory graduate college? Of course I will always have the memories. What good parent doesn't have memories of their children? What hurts are the memories I will now never have, the dreams we had that are permanently left unfulfilled. We had so much more to do!

Some people told me, "It will get better." If this comes from someone who has never experienced this pain, you can't imagine the anger that goes through you. And if someone has been through it, they should wait until people ask if it gets better, because for a long time you're not sure if you even want to live.

Others have said, "I can't imagine." This is probably what's said the most, and it is said in all honesty because of course you can't. Who could? Leave this one to a discussion with friends and family when I am not there.

One of the hardest things to hear is anything that starts with, "You need to..." Really? Who are you to suggest what I need to do? Have you been here? Have you walked a day in these shoes? It's like someone who doesn't have children trying to give you parenting advice (and multiplying that feeling by infinity).

One final note on this: Give people plenty of time before attempting to get them to see things through your faith and beliefs. As much faith as you may have, and as much as it may comfort you, people just aren't in a receptive frame of mind when in the depths of grief.

What to Say to People in Their Pain

You want to know the best thing anyone ever said to me? After the accident, one of Cole's lacrosse travel team coaches, Paul, came up to me and simply said, "No words." I'll never forget that. I can't tell you how meaningful it was to me. It sounds so simple, maybe even empty. But it spoke to me in a way that nothing else could.

In those two words were conveyed everything I needed. It conveyed his understanding of how senseless it all was. It conveyed his understanding of my utter helplessness—that nothing anyone could ever say or do would ever bring Cole back. Most importantly, it conveyed, "I have no way to fix this, but I want you to know that I'm here for you in your suffering."

That's all anyone ever really wants—to hear, "I'm here for you." And that's usually conveyed more by actions than by words. I remember other experiences with my friends, Brian and Shelly, Laurie and Bryan, and Dave and Jennifer. They just sat and listened to me as I talked about Cole through tears. They never said a word, they were just there for me. I didn't realize until later how impactful that was for me.

Another helpful thing to comfort people in their grief is to leave short "I was just thinking about you" messages via cell phone or text. It seems simple, but they do mean more than you know. I know there were people who were frustrated when they didn't hear back from me during those first few months. But I received every message, and each one was meaningful to me, even if

I wasn't in a mental space to respond at the time. It is amazing how much energy it took to return a phone call during that time. When you left a message and asked, "How about dinner on Friday?", it was not personal that I didn't go. When I did start going out again, I had precious little energy to make an appearance.

I am not sure how many weeks it was before I was able to open all the cards and letters I received. It took a day and a half to open and read all of them. They meant so much I still have them all today. There were so many from those who didn't know me but knew Cole. I was taken aback by all I received from folks who knew neither of us but felt compelled to write.

I know how helpless it feels to be with someone going through a major life tragedy. But that feeling of helplessness comes from thinking we need to do something to fix the tragedy or make the pain go away. We can get rid of that feeling by understanding that that's not what people need and want—they simply want us to be there for them. And that's more than enough.

18

You Become Who You Spend Time With

"Tell me who your friends are and I will tell you who you are." —Greek Proverb

---

I used to harp a lot on Cole about his friends. I'd say things like, "Be careful who you're calling your friends. Be careful who you associate with." Because the saying is true, that we're judged by the company we keep. As George Washington said, "Associate yourself with men of good quality if you esteem your own reputation, for 'tis better to be alone than in bad company."

It's easy to get caught up with the wrong people who drag you down. A lot of high schoolers in particular find themselves in compromising situations and say things like, "Well, it wasn't my fault. I was with Johnny. He did it." Well, why were you with them to begin with? You have to take responsibility for all your choices along the way. And few choices are more important than whom you pick as your friends.

The Science Behind Choosing the Right Friends

Who you become tomorrow is largely determined by the friends you keep today. This isn't just theory—it's scientific.

Consider the research data discovered by Harvard professors Nicholas Christakis and James Fowler, which they detail in their book *Connected: How Your Friends' Friends' Friends Affect Everything You Feel, Think, and Do*:

- We are 61 percent more likely to smoke if we have a direct relationship with a smoker. If your friend of a friend is a smoker, you are 29 percent more likely to smoke. Even at a third degree of separation (friend of a friend's friend), you are 11 percent more likely.
- If you have a friend that becomes obese, the odds that you'll gain weight jump to 57 percent.
- A British study revealed that among binge drinkers, 54 percent reported that all or almost all of their friends are binge drinkers, compared to 15 percent of non-binge drinkers.
- One Harvard study found that Harvard students were 8.3 percent more likely to get a flu shot if an additional 10 percent of their friends got a flu shot.
- People who are surrounded by happy people have a significantly greater likelihood of future happiness.

It's just common sense that we tend to mirror the attitudes, emotions, likes, interests, and habits of our peers—"birds of a feather" and all that. As social critic Eric Hoffer put it, "When people are free to do as they please, they usually imitate each other." But underlying common sense is a fascinating biological mechanism in the human brain, which scientists call the "mirror neuron system."

Christakis and Fowler explain:

Our brains practice doing actions we merely observe in others, as if we were doing them ourselves. If you've ever watched an intense fan at a game, you know what we are talking about— he twitches at every mistake, aching to give his own motor actions to the players on the field.

When we see players run, jump, or kick, it is not only our visual cortex or even the part of our brain that thinks about what we are observing that is activated, but also the parts of our brain that would be activated if we ourselves were running, jumping, or kicking...

It seems we are always poised to feel what others feel and do what others do.

We're biologically built to take on the qualities with those whom we associate with the most. If you want to know how your life will turn out in the next five to ten years, just consider the lives and trajectories of your friends. That will reveal how you'll turn out perhaps more than any other factor.

> "Be careful the environment you choose for it will shape you; be careful the friends you choose for you will become like them."
> —*W. Clement Stone*

How to Choose the Right Friends

The wrong friends don't have your best interests at heart. They're in it only for what you can offer them. They drag you down and bring out the worst in you. They make you feel bad about yourself. They don't like to see you succeed because it makes them jealous.

Most people want to see you be successful right up to the level where they are. In other words, very few "friends" will ever cheer you on past the level they are at in life.

> "Choose your friends wisely—they will make or break you." —*J. Willard Marriott*

In contrast, the right friends focus on what they contribute to the relationship. They sincerely care about you. They bring out the best in you and boost your self-esteem. They help you succeed, and celebrate your successes with you.

In my presentations to high school students I use the following acronym to help them choose the right friends. True friends are people who:

F — Fight for you.

R — Respect you.

I — Include you.

E — Encourage you.

N — Need you.

D — Deserve you.

S — Stand by you.

Thomas J. Watson counseled, "Don't make friends who are comfortable to be with. Make friends who will force you to lever yourself up." If you want a successful life, hang out with success-minded people.

PART IV

Be a Servant Leader

In his book, *Journey to the East*, Herman Hesse tells the story of a group of travelers who were served by Leo, who did their menial chores and lifted them with his spirit and song. All went well until Leo disappeared one day. The travelers fell into disarray and could go no farther. The journey was over.

Years later, one of the travelers saw Leo again— as the revered head of the Order that sponsored the journey. Leo, who had been their servant, was the titular head of the Order, a great and noble leader.

Author and thought leader Robert Greenleaf read this story and saw in it the most important factor of great leadership: service. He coined the phrase "servant leader." In *The Servant as Leader*, Greenleaf explained, "...this story clearly says—the great leader is seen as servant first, and that simple fact is the key to his greatness. Leo was actually the leader all of the time, but he was servant first because that was what he was, deep down inside.

"Leadership was bestowed upon a man who was by nature a servant. It was something given, or assumed, that could be taken away. His servant nature was the real man, not bestowed, not assumed, and not to be taken away. He was servant first."

True leaders aren't driven by the desire to boss others or to be recognized. Rather, they are driven by the desire to serve. Thus, anyone in any position or station of life can be a leader by serving others.

19

Be Coachable

"Discipline and diligence are up there on the list, but one of the most important qualities of many really successful people is humility. If you have a degree of humility about you, you have the ability to take advice, to be coachable, teachable. A humble person never stops learning." —*Todd Blackledge, former NFL quarterback*

One of Cole's defensive coaches, Al, told me a story about Cole that always makes me laugh. Al was in his '50s and was one of the more disciplinarian coaches Cole had. He didn't speak much, but when he needed to, the guys listened.

One time Cole's team was playing against a team they should have been beating easily, but they weren't playing well. The kids' heads just weren't in the game. At halftime, Al felt like he need to "get into these guys and give them a chewing out," as he put it to me. So he said his piece, but he felt like it didn't really land with a lot of the kids. Immediately afterward, Al started regretting it a bit, wondering if he had gone too far.

After his speech, as the team was running back onto the field, Cole came up to Al, patted him on the butt, and said, "Coach, well said. I got what you were saying. Half of them got it, the other half didn't. They all need to hear it again."

They ended up rallying and finishing strong to win the game.

Don't Take Anything Personally

That story is so funny to me because what kid his age does that? This is a well-respected coach who's about the same age as his father, who just went off on the whole team. Cole felt comfortable enough to pat a coach the age of his father on the butt to basically affirm to him that he had said the right thing. Most kids would have responded to that by taking it personally and being defensive: "It wasn't me. I work hard. I'm busting my butt. Don't yell at me." But that was never Cole. Cole was always so coachable, so willing to listen and learn. He had such an admirable humility about him that played a huge role in his success.

I asked Al if he could remember any time when Cole complained. He answered, "No, never."

I said, "Isn't that rare in your experience as a coach?"

He answered, "Absolutely. I've coached young athletes for fifteen years and he's a kid who always sticks out in my mind. You're never supposed to have favorites, but if I had to list the kids that had an impact on me, Cole would be at the top of the list."

Another of his coaches, Ryan, told me, "I loved coaching Cole because I could say whatever I wanted to and he wouldn't take offense. He trusted me. His attitude was always, 'You're the coach, you know better than I do, and you just want to help me get better.'"

Cole's high school English teacher, Mike McIntyre, added, "Cole not only listened to advice, but he would actually use it and apply it to the best of his ability. He was always open to feedback. A lot of high school students get upset when they get a bad grade and they want to blame the teacher, but Cole never perceived it that way. He genuinely wanted to learn and do his best, and he would use feedback to improve."

One of the greatest enemies of success is taking things personally. So many people have a chip on their shoulder. They don't want to take advice from anyone because it hurts their pride. They want to believe that they've got everything figured out and that no one can teach them anything.

Conversely, one of the greatest contributors of success is a humble attitude. With humility, you don't take anything personally. You're not constantly on the defensive. Rather, you're open and willing to listen. You may not take everyone's advice, but you're at least open to hearing it. You don't take offense when someone tries to teach you something, even if it's not delivered kindly.

When we learn the lesson to never take anything personally, we open our minds and hearts to learning like never before. We realize that *everyone* has something to teach us. No matter how people deliver their messages, we take it in stride and use it to become a better person.

We also realize that any time anyone seems to be upset with us, it's more about them than it is about us. As Don Miguel Ruiz explained in his book, *The Four Agreements*:

> Nothing other people do is because of you. It is because of themselves. All people live in their own dream, in their own mind; they are in a completely different world from the one we live in. When we take something personally, we make the assumption that they know what is in our world, and we try to impose our world on their world.
>
> Even when a situation seems so personal, even if others insult you directly, it has nothing to do with you. What they say, what they do, and the opinions they give are according to the agreements they have in their own minds…
>
> When you take things personally, then you feel offended, and your reaction is to defend your beliefs and create conflicts. You make something big out of something so little, because you have the need to be right and make everybody else wrong.

And it's not just about not taking offense from individual people, but also not taking offense at life itself when it's trying to teach us. For example, one time Cole's travel team played in the MVP Tournament at the University of Delaware. It was one of the best tournaments they had ever played, with the best competition they had played against. Many of the players they played against had already committed to top NCAA Division I schools. Two weeks after this tournament, a lot of the kids they played against competed in an All-American game on ESPN, which Cole and I watched on TV.

There was one game in particular during this tournament where Cole had not played well. Where he typically would win 80 percent of his face-offs, in this game he won maybe 50 percent. Many of his offensive and defensive moves that typically dominated opponents just weren't working that well. As we were walking off the field, I started congratulating him and telling him what he did well in an effort to lift his spirits.

He stopped me cold, looked at me, and said, "What game were you watching?"

It was a great lesson to me in humility, and about accepting the lessons of life. He was realistic about his abilities and performance. He didn't get mad at anyone or anything outside of himself. He didn't take it personally. Rather, he simply took it as another lesson, which he could use to improve himself and his game. When we experience failure, we can either get better or get bitter, and taking things personally is a sure-fire way to get bitter.

The more we take things personally, the less coachable we are. And the less coachable we are, the less we can learn. The most successful people are those who are constantly learning. And that starts with being coachable.

The Best Leaders are Great Followers

Successful people are leaders. But before they become good leaders, they first learn how to be good followers.

Barbara Kellerman, a leadership lecturer at Harvard University, explains there is a lot a person can learn about being a good leader by being a good follower.[13] Good followers, she says, are passionately committed and deeply involved. They actively support good leaders, while bad followers do little to contribute to the team.

Good followers learn to "read" their colleagues, co-workers, customers, and other audiences. They understand what motivates them and what upsets them. Good followers also learn important diplomacy skills, like the ability to get along well with others despite any differences. They are great collaborators. They help their leaders and their teams achieve goals.

"Great followers understand that public loyalty leads to private influence." –Michael Hyatt

Good followers are also courageous. Kellerman notes that good followers can aid the leader when he or she is doing the right thing—but they also have to have the courage to stand up to the leader if he or she is doing something wrong.

In contrast, bad followers sabotage team goals. They tend to be lazy and selfish. They don't work well with others. They go along with poor decisions and don't stand up to poor leaders, even when they know they should say or do something.

When you consider the qualities of a good follower, you find that they're the same qualities of a good leader. As former HP executive vice president Vyomesh Joshi said, "The key to being a great leader was to practice good followership."[14] In other words, leaders who have been good followers and who practice good followership principles understand how to work with people to bring out the best in them.

You can't become an effective leader until you learn to be an effective follower. You can't give orders with credibility if you're not willing to take orders. If you want to become a leader and succeed, it starts with being coachable.

20

The Silent Leader

> "A leader is best when people barely know he exists, when his work is done, his aim fulfilled, they will say: we did it ourselves." —*Lao Tzu*

Cole's coach, Al, whom I mentioned in the previous chapter, knew Cole from the time he was about ten years old. He worked with Cole a lot and saw how he interacted with his team. When I interviewed him to get his insights for this book, he used a phrase to describe Cole that really stuck out to me: He called Cole a "silent leader."

I asked him to explain what he meant by that and he said:

He wasn't very vocal, and he didn't need to be. For example, if the other players were slacking off during practice or a game, or maybe complaining about doing extra sprints, that seemed to drive him even more. He wouldn't complain, he wouldn't say anything to them. He would take it upon himself to dig in and work harder. He would inspire the other players with his actions, not his words. He led by example. I saw how it fueled his teammates. They would look at him and say, 'We're complaining, but Cole's not—he's working his tail off.'

If somebody was dogging it, then he would pat them on the back and encourage them. One time I remember we were running sprints and one of the kids was a lot slower than everyone else. He was the last one on the field finishing his sprints. Cole ran out on the field and ran with him—and he had already finished his own sprints.

I remember a heated game where one of our players took a cheap shot. Cole was the first one over there to pull him up. Another of our players started getting into a fight. Cole didn't say anything, but just pulled the guy away.

Cole just always had that presence that we could all count on. He was the one everyone looked to for leadership, whether he was a captain or not, or whether he even said anything or not.

I know from my own experience that this is true as well. He was such a presence to me in my life. He was more than an example to his teammates on the field—

he was an example to me. I learned so much about how to live and lead from him.

You Don't Need a Title to Lead

Effective leadership isn't about roles or titles. It's about a frame of mind, a quality of the soul. The best leaders don't pull rank. They don't badger or berate. They don't force people to do what they want. Rather, they earn the right to lead through their example. They put in the long, hard hours of personal effort. They strive for excellence. They never give up.

And their best leadership comes not through their words, but through their actions. It is the "silent leaders," not the brash tyrants, who exert the greatest influence.

Here are the qualities of silent leadership, which Cole demonstrated so well:

Example

Silent leaders recognize they cannot ask someone to do a task that they themselves wouldn't do or haven't done. They set the example for others to follow. Silent leaders hold themselves to the same (or higher) standard than they hold for others.

Humility

Silent leaders show humility in times of success and times of failure. They know it takes a team to accomplish great feats. They take constructive criticism well because they see failure as an opportunity to grow.

Trust

Silent leaders do not micromanage or nag others. They demonstrate confidence in others by trusting them to complete the work that has been assigned to them.

Follow-Through

Silent leaders do what they say they are going to do. They back up the talk with action. They finish projects they started.

Calmness

Silent leaders are composed and confident, even in the midst of chaos. Through reflective preparation, they are able to keep cool in different scenarios.

Unselfishness

The goal of silent leaders isn't to aggrandize themselves, but rather to lift each member of the team, and to accomplish mutual goals as a team. They sacrifice personal benefit for the good of all.

Listening

By allowing everyone to contribute, silent leaders distribute ownership to the group. When people have a stake in the group, they are more willing to participate and work hard to ensure the group succeeds. Effective listening means everyone is heard and his or her ideas actually have the opportunity to be considered. Listening doesn't mean waiting for your turn to speak.

Jim Breslawski is the president of my company, Henry Schein Inc., and he's a perfect example of being a great listener. Here's a guy who's at the top and wouldn't have to be a good listener if he didn't want to be. But ask anyone who has ever met him and they will tell you he's the best listener you'd ever want to meet. And I know that his listening skill has been a key factor in his success.

Self-Awareness

At Ronald Reagan's funeral, Margaret Thatcher gave a tribute to him in which she described what made him a great president in her opinion: "Ronald Reagan knew his own mind, he had firm principles, and I believe right ones, he expounded them clearly, he acted upon them decisively."

Silent leaders "know their own minds," and in order to do that, they cultivate self-awareness. They are not swayed by the crowd, but rather listen to the voice of conscience and stand firm in their principles.

The Heart of Leadership is Service

Curt and Traci are among my closest friends. Curt was also one of Cole's coaches when he was younger. They echoed Al's thoughts and told me:

> There was a lot of caring in Cole's heart for every kid in the lacrosse program. He recognized that some kids weren't able to play, but they really wanted to learn. And he pushed them to get better.

As they all started moving into high school, it became very apparent that if you got a point across to Cole—which didn't take much—he absorbed it and immediately started pushing it down to the other players. And he would show almost similar excitement or frustrations that coaches would have watching the kids as they developed. It was almost more like he was a part-time coach as a player.

Cole was always the guy on the team who was helping others to get better. He was the one people could depend on to help them whenever they needed it. He taught through his example that the best thing any leader can do is serve people.

~~~~~~~~~~~~~~~~~~~~~~~

"I long to do great and noble things. But it is my destiny to do small things in great and noble ways." –*Helen Keller*

~~~~~~~~~~~~~~~~~~~~~~~

In his book, *Servant Leadership*, Robert Greenleaf explained:

The servant-leader is servant first...It begins with the natural feeling that one wants to serve, to serve first. Then conscious choice brings one to aspire to lead. That person is sharply different from one who is leader first, perhaps because of the need to assuage an unusual power drive or to acquire material possessions...

The difference manifests itself in the care taken by the servant-first to make sure that other people's highest priority needs are being served. The best test, and difficult to administer, is: Do those served grow as persons? Do they, while being served, become healthier, wiser, freer, more autonomous, more likely themselves to become servants? And, what is the effect on the least privileged in society? Will they benefit or at least not be further deprived?

Servant leaders focus not on themselves, but rather on the people on their teams and in their communities. They don't care who gets the credit, as long as the team accomplishes shared goals. (This is exactly why Cole was so well respected on the field and why all his teammates looked up to him so much.)

If you want to become a leader and make a difference for others, you don't need to be powerful and boisterous. You don't need to be super intelligent or talented. You don't need a title or prestige. All you need is to learn how to serve others. Far too many people think, "It's not my job," rather than, "How can I help?" Your success in your career and your entire life is entirely dependent on your service to others.

21

Performers Look Good, Leaders Help Everyone Else Look Good

~~~~~~~~~~~~~~~~

*"When we seek to discover the best in others,
we somehow bring out the best in ourselves."*
—*William Arthur Ward*

~~~~~~~~~~~~~~~~

In Chapter 12 I told you the story of how Cole leaped at the opportunity to take face-offs for his lacrosse team, and how he then became one of the best face-off players in the state of Wisconsin. Well, there's more to that story.

When Cole was a senior, I was at one of his games, leaning against the fence on the track watching the team go through warm-ups. I heard a voice behind me say, "Excuse me, are you Cole Philhower's dad?"

I turned around and said to the couple standing there, "Yes, I am."

They introduced themselves as Tim and Wendy Scott. (They've since become very close friends of mine.)

Tim said, "I just want to say what a great son you have. It's so wonderful that he's teaching Isaac face-offs." Isaac is their son, and he was a sophomore at the time. He was a fantastic athlete in lacrosse, football, and track.

I had no idea that this had been going on. Later, I heard a lot more about it. My friend Curt knew about it, and he told me, "What amazed me about Cole is that, after he had developed his skill with face-offs, you would think that he would want to take every face-off he could. But when Isaac expressed an interest in learning face-offs, he took him under his wing and worked hard with him. It was to the point where he pushed Isaac and would tell him, 'You need to get better so you can beat me and get on the field.' He told Isaac at one point, 'My goal is to make you the best face-off guy we can.'"

I was astounded. Who does that? The face-off position is such a coveted position. And here he was, working with Isaac, an underclassman with the sincere intention of helping Isaac become better than he was at face-offs.

Isaac said of Cole, "Cole was someone that I could look to for help on the team and who was always so willing to help me to become the best player. It was so helpful to have someone like Cole to make me better. Cole was one of the most selfless people I knew, he cared about the success of his team more than his own personal success."

You'd think I'd stop being astounded by these types of stories about Cole, because that was just his nature. But every time I hear one it's just amazing to me what a great kid he was.

After Cole's accident, Curt told me yet another story about him that I never knew. Curt used to run a lot of lacrosse summer camps for young kids who had never tried lacrosse to introduce them to the sport. He told me, "Cole never missed a single one of those camps. With Cole, I had an instant assistant coach everywhere I went. He was always there and he always helped to clean up.

"And he had those kids wrapped around his finger. He would take the lacrosse ball and snap it over his shoulder and hit the net from almost any angle, and the eyes on those seven- and eight-year-old kids would pop out. It was fantastic to have him around."

On top of that, if any of those kids couldn't get a ride to the camp, he would pick them up. This wasn't anything he was required to do. It was all volunteer time. I did tell him he should be a part of the camps and to always give back. I told him that for those who have been given a lot, much is expected. However, I never knew he never missed a camp, and there were a few camps every summer.

Another of Cole's teammates and friends, Trevor, told me another story about Cole that I never knew. Both of them had been getting looked at by college coaches and recruiters. In one college recruiting tournament in particular, where they were playing some top-rated teams on the east coast, they both had a great opportunity to be seen by recruiters. Trevor and Cole were the "clear" for their team, meaning after a turnover the two of them would work the ball back and forth to move it up the field.

Trevor said, "We were Wisconsin kids who weren't even supposed to be up there with the caliber of these teams. But Cole wasn't fazed by it. One game he pulled me aside and told me, 'Hey, I'm going to pull your guy away from you, then get you the ball and you just take it.' We did that all game, and I was able to pull off some really great shots because of that. Because of my shots that day, after the game three or four college coaches gave me their cards. I never would have had those shots had Cole not set me up so selflessly. The whole point of those tournaments was to be seen by recruiters. And Cole did all the hard work and the plays that allowed me to shine."

Trevor was a defenseman, and defensive players can't cross the mid-field without a penalty unless a middie, like Cole, stays back. Cole was good enough to defend, which allowed Trevor the opportunity to go downfield and shoot. Defensemen rarely get an opportunity to shoot. Trevor was able to shoot that game because Cole stayed back and gave him that opportunity.

Again, in a world where most teenagers tend to be so self-serving, who does that? But that was Cole.

Lift Everyone Around You

So many people blow out other peoples' light so that they can shine brighter. They assume that if they lift others around them, they'll lose status. But nothing could be further from the truth. The more you help others, the more others want to help you. It's just a natural law. Sure, a few people may take advantage of you. But whatever you give always comes back to you in the long run.

What matters most isn't how good you look, but how good you make everyone around you look. As we learned in the comparison between Ryan Leaf and Peyton Manning, your team's winning record matters much more than your personal stats.

Another athlete we could highlight to make this point is Allen Iverson. Iverson was a sensational, superstar basketball player by any measure. At just six feet tall and weighing only 165 pounds, during his fourteen-year career in the NBA, he scored 24,368 points, which places him at #19 on the all-time scorer list. He averaged 27 points per game, 6.2 assists per game, and 2.2 steals per game. He won the Rookie of the Year award in 1997. He was an NBA All-Star in eleven seasons and won the All-Star game MVP award twice. He was the leading NBA scorer in four seasons (only three players have won four scoring titles). Yet despite his individual success, he never won what matters most: a championship ring.

This could be attributed to a lot of factors. But mostly, he was simply a selfish player. Ironically, his personal stats could have been even better, had he learned some humility and teamwork. But after ten years in Philadelphia, he bounced around in the league and never found another home because of his "alpha-dog" style—if he couldn't be *the* star, he wasn't interested in playing. As sports writer Michael Kaskey-Blomain said, "Accepting his own, potentially diminished role within the league's altering landscape was something that

Iverson was unwilling or unable to do. His statistics, as well as his legacy in the league, suffered because of it."[15] Sports writer Dan Podheiser put it succinctly: "Iverson was the ultimate 'me' player."[16]

In contrast to Iverson, all of the great basketball players who have ever won championships learned how to play with a team. They knew they couldn't get it done alone, that a championship is won with all members of the team playing at their full potential. Bill Russell, for example, holds the record for winning the most championships in the NBA—eleven total. He expressed the mindset of a true champion when he said, "The most important measure of how good a game I played was how much better I'd made my teammates play."

At some point in life, we all have to decide whether we want to be a player who racks up stats and personal glory, or a player who wins championships. We have to choose between being a personal performer or a team leader. Because it's always the true leaders, who help others around them shine, who win championships. As sculptor Gary Lee Price said, "They rise highest who lift as they go."

PART V

Enjoy Life by Being Present

We've talked a lot about setting goals and working hard to achieve them. But the drive to achieve can actually become misplaced and misguided. We can become so obsessed with winning, accomplishing, and achieving that we fail to slow down and notice the most important things that are right in front of our faces all the time.

We need goals in order to live life on purpose. But we can't get so focused on goals in the future that we miss the beauty of each moment in the present. We can't focus so much on accomplishing tasks that we neglect the most important thing: connecting with people. As mindfulness teacher Jack Kornfield said, "When we get too caught up in the busyness of the world, we lose connection with one another—and ourselves." We have to find that balance between striving for goals and simply being in the moment.

The present moment is all we ever have. A life well lived is about maximizing our peace, joy, and fulfillment in each moment. And the most important way to do that is by cultivating and building close relationships with the people who matter most to us.

22

CHAPTER TWENTY-TWO

What are We Waiting For?

"Things which matter most must never be at
the mercy of things which matter least."

—*Johann Wolfgang von Goethe*

When Cole was about in third grade, his bus stop was just across the street from our house. The bus would arrive at about 6:30 in the morning. In cold weather, he'd be all bundled up and he and a few other kids would huddle around for a few minutes until the bus arrived.

I don't know why it took me so long to do it. But one morning it was unusually cold, even for Wisconsin, and as he was heading out to the bus stop, I told him, "Hey bud, just hop in the car with me and I'll take you over there." I turned right out of my driveway, drove seventy yards, turned into my neighbor's driveway, backed out, parked, and waited for the bus to top the small hill. We sat there talking until the bus arrived. It kept him warm and, even though it was only a few minutes, it was great bonding time.

At the time I thought to myself, "Why does it have to be 0 degrees in the middle of winter for me to do this with my son every day?"

From then on, every day for the next year and a half until his bus route changed, this became a daily routine for us. We'd hop in the car a bit early, pull up to the bus stop, and sit there talking until the bus arrived. We did it whether it was snowing or sunny, whether it was December or May. I wondered if parents who saw us wondered, "What kind of spoiled brat is this kid?"

It was such a small thing that you're probably wondering why I'm even bringing it up. Yet it was so meaningful to me. It was such a simple way to connect with Cole, to show him that he was my most important priority, even in my busy work days.

And it was a great lesson to me to stop waiting to do the most important things in life.

"The life you have left is a gift. Cherish it. Enjoy it now, to the fullest. Do what matters, now."

—*Leo Babauta*

Get Clear on What's Most Important

I think most of us give a lot of lip service to saying our families and close relationships are the most important things in our lives. But do our actions really reflect that? If people were to measure how we spend our time, would they believe us?

It's important to set goals and strive to reach them. But all our goals must be placed within the context of our core values. To paraphrase the late leadership guru Stephen Covey, what if we climb the ladder of our goal, only to find that we had it leaning against the wrong wall? Or as D.L. Moody put it, "Our greatest fear should not be that we won't succeed, but that we will succeed at something that doesn't matter."

And there are many things that do matter in life, but that must be put into a bigger perspective. For example, a lot of people would give almost anything to become the golf champion that Jack Nicklaus was. But he was able to put golf into its proper perspective. As he said in a speech once, "I look to golf as a game. I never wanted golf to dominate my life. Golf was my vehicle to make a living, but (wife Barbara and I) felt that our family was by far the most important thing."[17]

Likewise for me, Cole was the most important part of my life. I was also thankful that my company supported my efforts to be there for Cole. Our national sales meeting is always held around the first week of June each year. It's a huge event for our company, and one that a corporate director like me wouldn't dream of missing. But Cole's senior year, it was graduation weekend and it just so happened that the event also coincided with the Wisconsin state lacrosse tournament, which is played over the last two weeks of high school. I was usually able to attend the tournament, then go straight to the national sales meeting. But this year I had to choose.

If I were to go to the sales meeting, I would miss not only the end games of the state tournament, but also Cole's last week of high school. Of course, I wasn't about to miss either. Fortunately, my company understood. In fact, Tim, the president of our division, knew I was struggling with not going to the sales meeting. One day he stuck his head in my office and assured me I was doing the right thing (which says so much about our company's culture).

Cole's team won their first game of the tournament on Tuesday, then lost their second game, the quarter final, on Thursday evening. (Unfortunately, Cole was unable to play that game, as he had walking pneumonia, which developed into mono.) As I was driving west on Highway 94 towards Madison before the game, I started to get emotional with the realization that Cole's high school career was over. I said to myself over and over again, "I couldn't have done any more. I couldn't have been there more." I had lived every important moment with Cole from grade school to that point—every practice, every school event, parent teacher meetings, car rides, traveling the world with Cole, so many dinners at Applebee's with he and his friends.

You've heard the classic saying that no one on their deathbed has ever wished that they had spent more time at the office. Yet sadly, that realization doesn't come for many people until they *are* on their deathbeds. Failure is not falling short of one's goals. It is the result of pursuing the wrong goals for the wrong reasons.

Before setting goals, we must get super clear on what's most important to us. For example, if our family is most important to us and we set a goal to become a millionaire, what happens when those two values conflict? Will we find ourselves getting sucked into working eighty-hour weeks and neglecting our family? Or will we keep our family our priority? My life was Cole and my career. I did my best to keep them in that order.

That which we give our energy to grows. Conversely, that which we neglect decays. If we want the most important things in our lives to flourish, we must give them proper energy. We must constantly check ourselves to make sure our energy expenditures reflect our deepest values and purest desires.

Learn to Say "No"

It's hard to stay on track with our core values because life is so full of distractions. Prosperity and technology have given us so many ways to spend our time. We're swimming in opportunity. There are so many directions we can take on a daily basis. There is so much competing for our time and energy.

One of the most valuable skills we can develop in today's world is the ability to say "no." As billionaire Warren Buffet said, "The difference between successful people and really successful people is that really successful people say no to almost everything." The first step is to have a crystal-clear vision of who we are, what we value most, and who we want to become. This creates a standard by which all distractions and opportunities are measured. With that standard, opportunities become easy to judge and filter through.

Harry E. Fosdick explained, "No steam or gas drives anything until it is confined. No Niagara is ever turned into light and power until it is tunneled. No life ever grows great until it is focused, dedicated and disciplined." If we want a great life that really reflects our core values, we must learn to focus our time and energy on what matters most. We must learn to clear our schedules and carve out time for those things that are most important to us, yet that are so easy to neglect.

"The mark of a great man is one who knows when to set aside the important things in order to accomplish the vital ones." —*Brandon Sanderson*

Live by Design, Not by Default

I don't think anyone consciously sets out to stray from their values. What happens is that we stop paying attention, and then we start drifting.

A friend of mine once told me a story about drifting. He had been swimming a mile every day for months. One time he and his wife were staying on a lake. It looked to be about a half mile across, and he was pretty confident that he could swim across and back. What he didn't realize was that swimming in an indoor pool was dramatically different than swimming in open water.

He couldn't see more than two feet in front of him. Every time he came up for air, waves slapped his face, making him choke. *But the hardest challenge was not being able to swim in a straight line.* He had fixed his eyes on a large white rock across the lake as his goal. At first he tried taking fifty strokes before checking his progress. But he found that he was veering considerably to either side each time.

The only way he could stay on track was by looking up at his goal and recalibrating as necessary every twenty strokes instead. Thus, his progress was slow and tedious. But without constantly checking his progress, he never would have made it.

All too often, we put our heads down and swim through life without periodically checking to see if we're headed the right way. After years of hard work and largely thoughtless routines, we raise our heads and realize we've been swimming in the wrong direction. Even the most focused and committed must continually reconnect with their ultimate vision and most meaningful objectives to stay on track.

Similar to my friend's swimming experience, airplanes are off course 99 percent of the time. The pilot, using his instruments, must continually bring the plan back on course so that it arrives on schedule at its destination. You are the pilot of your life. To reach your destination, you must first of all determine what that destination will be by setting and writing down goals. Then, as you move toward your goals, you must make continual course corrections. Just as an airplane faces headwinds, downdrafts, storm fronts, wind shear, lightning and unexpected turbulence, you will experience obstacles in the pursuit of your goals. You must adapt and adjust accordingly.

Without conscious, consistent effort, we drift on the waves of social pressure and casual habits and drown in purposeless routines. The only way to achieve our purpose is to constantly recalibrate our thoughts and actions to our vision and objectives. It starts with getting clear on what's most important to us.

23

It's the Little Things that Matter Most

"It's not a big thing, but it's a thing— and they all add up." —Jim Philhower

In his book, *A Path with Heart*, mindfulness teacher Jack Kornfield tells the story of a man who was already rich in his late thirties. His thriving construction company paid for his expansive ranch, upscale town house, elegant sailboat, sleek BMW, and all the toys and experiences he could dream of.

Until one day, while driving, he blacked out. Tests revealed a fast-growing cancerous brain tumor. The doctor told him they had to operate immediately, and he had an agonizing choice to make: Since the tumor was in his brain's speech and comprehension center, if they were to operate, there was a chance he would lose his ability to read, write, speak, or understand any language. But if they didn't operate, he would have only six weeks to live. He had twenty-four hours to make the decision.

His sister called a spiritual advisor to visit with him. They sat and had a heartfelt conversation. Then he became silent. After a while of reflection, he turned to the spiritual advisor and said, "I've had enough of talking. Maybe I've said too many words. This evening it seems so precious just to have a drink of tap water or to watch the pigeons on the windowsill fly off in the air. They seem so beautiful to me. It's magic to see a bird go through the air. I'm not finished with this life. Maybe I'll just live it more silently."

The allure of being rich and famous is something that tugs at all of us. Our deepest longing is to *be* someone—someone who really matters, someone who accomplishes great things and is remembered after we are gone.

"Enjoy the little things in life, for one day you may look back and realize they were the big things." —*Robert Breault*

The unfortunate side effect of this perspective is that it easily misses the mark. In striving for greatness, hustling to live an extraordinary life, we often miss the beauty and joy of ordinary living. In our zeal to grasp the big things, we miss the little things that matter most.

What I Miss Most

You'd think that what I would miss the most about being with Cole would be the big things: big vacations we took, his college recruiting trips, watching him win big games, etc. But what I miss the most are the little things, which I never took for granted.

Every year, Cole and I used to get wood for our wood-burning fireplace at a place not far from our house. They have a massive wood splitter that can split huge logs. We used to watch it together. I still remember the sound it made. Then we'd load up the truck together.

I used to regularly leave money on the breakfast bar for Cole, just a few bucks. He'd write me thank-you notes. Every time I traveled for work, I'd always pick up some little gift for Cole. When he was younger, it was collectible keychains, and he ended up with a huge collection of them. Later, it was t-shirts, then paraphernalia from local college teams. Every airport I flew into, as soon as I got off the plane I would peek into gift shops on my way to baggage claim to see what I might pick up for Cole on my way back home. It was just a little thing to let him know I was thinking of him.

I used to buy Gatorade for him every time I went to the store, or when we would go together. We enjoyed going to the store together. Of course, what I miss more than anything is watching him play lacrosse. I was always so excited to just watch him run and play on the field. I could spot Cole on the field just by his gait and the way he carried himself. The most important times in our lives were the meals and conversations at our breakfast bar.

I remember one time in March, when Cole was a senior, Kettle Moraine was playing in a preseason tournament, about two and a half hours north of our town. Cole had injured his wrist the week before in another tournament, so he wasn't going to play in this one. But since he was a team leader, he met the team at the high school at 5:30 a.m. that Saturday morning and rode the bus with them to the tournament.

By this time, Cole had committed to play lacrosse at Benedictine University, which is about two and a half hours south of us in Chicago. That evening Benedictine had a home game against Hanover, another college that had also recruited Cole to play. Since Cole wasn't able to compete in the tournament, I asked his head coach if I could pick Cole up during the tournament and take him home. I left my house mid-morning, drove north to pick Cole up, then we drove the five hours back south to watch Benedictine beat Hanover. By the time we stopped to eat, it was almost 10:00 p.m. We stopped at a nice sports bar just north of Chicago. We bumped into one of Cole's favorite referees there.

I drove 505 miles that day. But it was a beautiful sunny spring Saturday and there was no other place I would have rather been. That day really was a microcosm of our life together.

Who will I leave money for in the morning now? Who will I buy silly little keychains for? Who will I watch play lacrosse? Who will I give advice too and talk to? All those little things are gone now. I can't even begin to tell you how meaningful they are.

Never Take the Little Things for Granted

As Cole entered high school, I had this vision of a teeter-totter in my head: His Freshman and Sophomore years would go by slower, then his Junior and Senior years would just fly by.

As corny as it sounds, all through Cole's senior year in high school I counted down the days I had left with him. Before he went to college, I would stop at the top of the stairs, stare into his bedroom at the #49, his lacrosse uniform number, which is painted on the wall above his headboard, and say the number of days I had left with him out loud before heading downstairs and off to work. Many days, instead of driving straight to work, I would leave a little early and head the opposite direction to the high school. I would stop at a little country store across the street from the high school and get a coffee or a sandwich and just stare at the school, thinking, "Only sixty-seven days left." "Only thirty-three days left." Those days counted down way too fast.

I never understood the parents who would say, "Only one more year and he/she is gone." "I have one left at home, then I am done" (as in, "I will be glad when they are out of the house"). I cherished every day. I never took one practice, one game, one trip of driving his friends home from practice, or our many dinners at Applebee's together for granted. I *so* looked forward to traveling around the country with him to tournaments, driving to away games, and, of course, walking into the high school stadium for home games. But what I miss most is just being with Cole, at our breakfast bar eating and talking, conversations in the car, just sharing and learning.

Recently at church, we were in the middle of a family series. The sermon that Sunday was on being present for your children. The pastor shared a story of disconnect between a father and son. The lesson was to make your children a priority and be there for them. It was a good sermon, but I must admit I found myself shaking my head and thinking, "I can't believe this needs to be taught."

From my perspective, I can promise you that there will come a time when you'll miss having your kids around. You're going to miss all the little things that you probably don't even notice right now. You're even going to miss all the things that bug you right now.

As country singer Trace Adkins sings in his song, "You're Gonna Miss This":

You're gonna miss this,
You're gonna want this back
You're gonna wish these days
Hadn't gone by so fast.
These are some good times,
So take a good look around
You may not know it now
But you're gonna miss this.

There's no question that you'll miss those little things. The real question, though, is whether or not you'll have regrets for not valuing those little things while you had them. If there is any consolation I have in Cole's death, it is that I wouldn't change anything in how I spent my time raising and being with Cole. I can't imagine how much more difficult this journey would be if I had to say, "I wish I had spent more time with Cole. I wish we would have done more together."

"If you were going to die soon and had only one phone call you could make, who would you call and what would you say? And why are you waiting?" —*Stephen Levine*

Make Every Day Your Last

Remember that man I mentioned with a brain tumor? He opted for the surgery. After fourteen hours of surgery he awoke to see his sister standing there and said, "Good morning." They were able to remove the tumor without losing his speech.

He recovered from his cancer and changed his entire life. He stopped being a workaholic and spent more time with his family. He became a counselor for others diagnosed with cancer and other terminal illnesses. He spent much of his time in nature and touching the lives of others.

Big houses, fancy cars, prestigious titles, and high-paying jobs that make us feel important are great. But life is about so much more than that. Life is about the ever-so-precious moments, which we so often take for granted. It's about the relationships that we often neglect until it's too late.

We spend so much time getting there that we rarely take time to bask in what we have. Life doesn't so much pass us by as we pass life by. In honor of Cole, I urge you to take stock of your life and make sure you're giving proper time and energy to what matters most. Make a greater effort to notice and enjoy the little moments. Because I can promise you this: There will come a time when you will give *everything* to have just one more moment...

24

Time Won't Stop

~~~~~~~~~~~~~~~~~~~~~~~~~~~~~~~~~

"Unfortunately, the clock is ticking, the hours are going by. The past increases, the future recedes. Possibilities decreasing, regrets mounting." — *Haruki Murakami*

~~~~~~~~~~~~~~~~~~~~~~~~~~~~~~~~~

Shortly after Cole's death, I received the following letter from one of his teachers:

Mr. James Philhower:

I write these words with great difficulty. I was Cole's English teacher during his sophomore and senior years for English 10 and English 101. I had the pleasure to see his tremendous growth in three short years. I remember Cole for having a healthy balance of playfulness and seriousness. He embodied the rare person who fully captures and appreciates what matters in almost everything he does.

Cole was magnetic, bright, and authentic. His charisma and charm emitted certain sincerity. He always lived in the moment, and upon hearing this tragic news, I couldn't help but think back to an essay Cole wrote last September. The assignment called for choosing a brief moment that had great significance, and Cole chose to write about saying goodbye to his college-bound friends at the end of last summer. The piece is poignant, and Cole chose his words carefully.

Cole's words move me. They show his love and devotion for those closest to him. I can see his smile, hear his laugh, and feel his sincerity as he pensively considered all that mattered most. These memories give me some solace, and I hope Cole's words help at some point during this time of tragedy.

My thoughts and prayers go out to you as you mourn the loss of such a special child. Please know how truly sorry I am.

Sincerely,

Michael McIntyre
English Teacher
Kettle Moraine High School

Mr. McIntyre included with his letter a copy of Cole's essay, which I had never read before. The title of it is, "Time Won't Stop for Me." He had no idea how right he was...

Below is Cole's essay, which obviously has so much meaning to me now. I hope you find meaning in it as well.

Time Won't Stop for Me

Cole Philhower
9/22/13

The night I said goodbye to my best friend was one I won't forget. Ever since I could remember, I was always hanging around with an older group of kids. I couldn't stand my class, so the pattern stuck with me up until my senior year. I was always running around with the grade above or below me, with the exception of some close friends in my 2014 class.

Summer was winding down, and all of last year's seniors, including my best friends, began to talk about college preparation and when they would be leaving. The thought hardly entered my mind that I would be losing a majority of my closest friends because they were all a year older than me. The thought would linger in the back of my mind, but nothing really hit me until I met with my group of best friends one last time.

The summer going into my senior year was the best summer I'd had. I was busy every day between lacrosse and hanging out with friends. We were always busy with our own errands during the day and would hang out when we could as late as we could. The nights just began to roll together and everyday was going by faster than the last. It was like our summer was one giant hangout that didn't stop for anything.

Until the last day actually came.

We didn't think much of it leading up to the last night I saw them. We'd just have casual conversations about who was rooming with who and where they'd be going to school, so at the time, I was hit with the awful realization that I wouldn't see many of the people closest to me for quite some time. Sure, they can come back on break and visit from time to time, but that just isn't the same.

When the last night finally came around, my best friends and I would do what was almost routine. We hung out for a few hours later on in the night like usual and met up with our other friends to figure out plans for what to do next. All of them started to talk about all of their memories and great times they had which prompted me to do the same.

I began to notice what kind of impact these guys had on my life. The places I went to, things I did and experienced were all with this group of guys that was going to continue on with their future as I was stuck with one more year to go.

When the time came for everyone to leave, I stood with my best friend and we both tried to avoid what we knew was coming. I looked at him and he looked back, we shook hands and pulled each other in for a hug while saying the same exact words: 'It's been real.' Those were the only words to sum up our experiences together, truly real, and it didn't surprise me that it was all we both said.

After I wished him luck, I got into my car and began to drive home. The quiet, dark drive kept me lost in thought, and I caught myself reminiscing about all of the best memories I had. I realized that time won't stand still just for me, and we all need to carry on with our futures regardless of what happens.

I'll always have the memories of everything we did, from playing under the warm summer sun to having parties where everyone felt at home because we were our own small family. Being able to look back on everything makes me appreciate it more than I did in the moment, and I can say those three words: It's been real.

What are We Doing to "Make it Real"?

Cole was more right in his essay than he ever could have known when he wrote it: Time didn't stop for him. Nor does it stop for any of us.

Have you ever heard country singer Tim McGraw's song, "Live Like You Were Dyin'"? It talks about a man diagnosed with something serious that "stopped [him] on a dime," after which he says, "I spent most of the next days, lookin' at the x-rays, talkin' 'bout the options and talkin' 'bout sweet time." What do you think about and what do you do when this happens? His answer is in the chorus:

> I went sky divin',
> I went rocky mountain climbin',
> I went 2.7 seconds on a bull name Fumanchu.
> And I loved deeper,
> And I spoke sweeter,
> And I gave forgiveness I've been denying,
> And he said someday I hope you get the chance,
> To live like you were dyin'.

I have to ask: Who *isn't* dying? Who on earth isn't getting closer to death with each and every living breath? *Why do we wait for a serious diagnosis before living life to the fullest?* We were born with the only diagnosis we need.

Every one of us is going to die. The only questions are when, and what do we choose to do about it. Like Cole said, what are we doing each and every day to "make it real"?

In his book, *Light on Enlightenment*, Christopher Titmuss gives us all some great questions to consider:

- Imagine it is your last day on earth. You have no tomorrow, no future. You can't do anything wild or insensitive.
- How would you spend your last day?
- What would you give attention to?
- What would you take time to observe?
- What would you appreciate or reflect upon?
- Now go ahead and do it before it is your last day!

I hope you get the chance to live like you were dying. Because you are.

PART VI

Leave a Legacy

The dictionary defines "legacy" as "a gift or a bequest, that is handed down, endowed or conveyed from one person to another." From its roots, it is often associated with money or property that is passed down from one generation to another.

But leaving a legacy is about far more than leaving material wealth—in fact, wealth is but a small fraction of one's true legacy. Leaving a legacy sharing not just what you have earned, but also what you have learned. It's about offering your talents and gifts to the world to make a meaningful and lasting contribution to humanity by serving a cause greater than yourself.

~~~~~~

Thinking in terms of leaving a legacy gives us a generational perspective. We focus on more than just what we can get out of life while we're here, but rather what we can give and what we can leave for others. We expand our awareness from selfish concerns to what benefits all of humanity. Legacy is the long-term product of a life well lived.

Cole left a legacy in the way that he lived his life and contributed value to others. He made a profound difference for me and for the world. May we all follow his example and leave our own legacy.

~~~~~~

25

The 49 Legacy

"Carve your name on hearts, not tombstones.
A legacy is etched into the minds of others and
the stories they share about you."

—*Shannon L. Alder*

Near Kettle Moraine High School, out by the lacrosse and football fields, there's a small hill, which is very visible from the county highway about 300 yards away. It used to be a tradition for graduating classes to drag big rocks onto the hill to form the shape of their graduation year. It was a big annoyance for the school, because the custodians had to mow around the rocks, so they would have to remove them.

In fact, it was such a big annoyance that at one point the school said, "This has to stop. If we find out who did it, you won't be able to walk across the stage to get your diploma." Nobody messed with the rocks after that threat and they stayed down for years. That is, until 2014.

Soon after Cole's accident, a bunch of Cole's friends worked through the night to carry rocks and put another number up on the hill. Except this time, the number wasn't a graduation year. It was the number 49, in honor of Cole. The high school retired Cole's jersey number the day of the accident, so no one will ever wear number 49 in lacrosse again.

Jeff Walters is the high school principal. I saw him at the funeral service and I said, "How about those rocks, Jeff? Looks pretty nice doesn't it?"

He said, "Yeah, Jim, I saw those."

And I just kept nodding my head and said, "So the school will take it down...never? Right, Jeff?"

And he smiled and said, "Jim, the school won't take it down."

"Thanks," I said. "I appreciate that."

The school didn't make any fuss about it. It stayed up for a week or two. Then, the custodians had to remove the rocks to mow the grass. They would roll them down the hill into a little gully just below it. As soon as they did it, the kids went back and put the 49 back up again. This happened a couple more times.

The next time the kids put the #49 rocks up, they spray painted them blue and gold (the high school colors). The number was huge and easily seen from the road. Again, the custodians would remove them to mow the grass, and then the kids would come and put them back up. This went on for about two-and-a-half years. I actually offered to pay the custodians to roll the rocks down the hill.

One hot summer day, I drove by the school and the rocks were down. I parked, walked down into the gully, grabbed a big rock, and hauled it up the hill. Then another and another. I spent the next couple hours hauling rocks under the hot sun, until I was exhausted. As I was working, a kid who looked to be about eleven or twelve years old walked past along the top of the hill and saw me working.

It wasn't long before that same kid showed up again. He asked me, "Hey, do you need any help?"

I said, "Yeah, would you mind?"

"No," he said, "I'll help you."

I looked up at the sky and said, "Cole, did you send him?"

I asked him what his name was and he said, "Will." Will rejuvenated me, and between the two of us we got the 49 back up that afternoon. I gave him whatever cash I had in my pocket, as well as one of my business cards. I told him, "Tell your mom that this is who you were with today, and this is who gave you the money." I've seen his mom a few times since and she always brings up that story.

The school never took the rocks down. But eventually, the custodians, who I'm sure didn't know anything about Cole, wised up and took the rocks away. But it was nice while it lasted, and I have faith the rocks will be back up someday.

I'm sure that little story doesn't mean much to you. But there is a point in me bringing it up: It's simply more evidence of the legacy Cole left. It shows how many people he touched and the good he did in the short time he was on this earth. He had such a positive influence on so many people. I'm not the only one who will remember #49 forever.

"There'll be two dates on your tombstone
and all your friends will read 'em
but all that's gonna matter is that little
dash between 'em." *–Kevin Welch*

What Will Be Your Legacy?

One of Stephen R. Covey's principles in his popular book, *The 7 Habits of Highly Successful People*, is "Begin with the End in Mind." To introduce the principle, he walks you through an exercise where you envision walking into a funeral parlor. You see the flowers and hear the organ music. You see the faces of friends and family. You walk to the front of the room and look into the casket. Inside, you see yourself. This is *your* funeral, and everyone here has come to honor you.

You sit down and the services proceed. There are four speakers: the first is from your family, the second is one of your friends, the third is from your work, and the fourth is from your church or community organization.

Covey writes, "Now think deeply. What would you like each of these speakers to say about you and your life? What kind of husband, wife, father or mother would you like their words to reflect? What kind of a son or daughter or cousin? What kind of friend? What kind of working associate?

"What character would you like them to have seen in you? What contributions, what achievements would you want them to remember? Look carefully at the people around you. What difference would you like to have made in their lives?"

They're powerful questions that each of us should ask on a regular basis. It's so easy to get caught up in the day-to-day grind that we don't pause to take stock of our lives, where we're headed, and what we're trying to accomplish. But as we've learned from Cole's life, life is so short. We've got one shot to make a difference.

Knowing we're here for just a short time, our focus should be not just on what we experience and accomplish during our lifetime, but also on what we can leave for future generations. As Wes Jackson said, "If your life's work can be accomplished in your lifetime, you're not thinking big enough."

The Cole Philhower Foundation

When I woke up the Sunday of the open house, two days after Cole's accident, my first thought was, "Dear God, this isn't a dream." My next thought was, "Cole's name has to live on forever at Kettle Moraine." He had done so much for so many kids, parents, coaches, and teachers. I wanted his spirit of contribution to live. I had the idea to create a foundation to serve underprivileged kids here. We have a hardship fund that parents can donate to for the kid's families who do not have the means to be able to pay for the lacrosse season fees. I always donated to the fund every year when I registered Cole to play.

That morning I thought, "Every kid who wants to play lacrosse here will be able to play." The first people who arrived at my house were my dear friends, Curt and Traci Disrud. (Incidentally, they were the original people who started the lacrosse program at our school.) Curt is also my CPA. I told them what I was thinking. I said, "I don't know how to go about this. Can you help?"

Curt just nodded, which meant, "Don't worry about it, Jim. I'll take care of it."

Within a week, Curt had done a lot of research. We decided how to structure the foundation and we got everything set up. The sole purpose of the foundation is to provide financial support in the way of college scholarships for high school seniors and for high school athletes to play lacrosse and other sports at Kettle Moraine. 100 percent of the proceeds from the foundation go directly to Kettle Moraine families. The foundation has awarded fifteen scholarships and $16,500 to college-bound seniors in its first three years. All donations are 100 percent tax-deductible.

Through conversations with friends, we created the Cole Philhower Leadership Award. The foundation gives it each year to the boys' varsity lacrosse player who best exemplifies the characteristics that defined Cole, what he stood for, how he treated teammates and coaches, and how he conducted himself overall. The head coach and his staff decide who wins the award. A $1,500 scholarship is included with the award. On the trophy for the award is engraved the acronym C.O.L.E., which stands for Commitment, Opportunity, Leadership, Excellence. It is awarded during the halftime ceremonies on senior night each year. The names of the winners are engraved on a memory plaque that is kept in the high school trophy case.

One winner of the award, Derek Hoppe, said, "Winning the Cole Philhower Leadership Award was a huge honor! Cole was such a huge role model and inspiration to the team and myself. I wanted to be a better person and teammate, and Cole made me realize that could happen. Winning his award brings me one step closer to being a better person like Cole."

I set up the foundation because Cole and I had a very blessed life, and not every kid has the same opportunities as Cole had to pursue their dreams. A lot of kids can't play lacrosse or other sports because of limited resources or lack of family support. Cole's foundation provides kids a pathway to higher education and more opportunities to play lacrosse. Not only will scholarships be awarded to student athletes, but also significant contributions will be made to the sports infrastructure and facilities at Kettle Moraine. For example, we're currently working on building a lacrosse wall for athletes to practice throwing balls against to increase hand-eye coordination and stick skills.

I mention the foundation because I want you to know that 100 percent of the profits from this book go to the foundation. I didn't write this book to make myself rich —I wrote it to honor Cole and to continue his legacy of service and contribution.

To learn more about the foundation and the work it's doing, please visit www.ColePhilhower.com.

Leave Your Mark

The singer Beyoncé sings a song called "I Was Here," which says:

I wanna leave my footprints on the sands of time

Know there was something that meant something that I left behind

When I leave this world, I'll leave no regrets

Leave something to remember, so they won't forget I was here I lived, I loved I was here

I did, I've done everything that I wanted

And it was more than I thought it would be

I will leave my mark so everyone will know I was here…

~~~~~~~~~~~~~~~

**"What we do for ourselves dies with us.
What we do for others and the world remains
and is immortal."** *–Albert Pike*

~~~~~~~~~~~~~~~

Cole left a legacy that will continue on in the lives of those he touched, and through his foundation. What legacy will *you* leave? What will be your mark on the world? What will you contribute that will last long after you are gone?

Just as I can never get Cole back, once you're gone, you're gone forever. But if you live consciously and wisely, your influence can be felt for generations.

26

Is This the Best I Can Do?

"We have to do the best we can. This is our sacred human responsibility." —Albert Einstein

By now you have a good idea of my love for Cole, so this may not even surprise you. But here's the thing: If I absolutely knew that by doing it I could go be with Cole and have our life again, I'd kill myself. I really would.

Anyone who's been through a similar tragedy can tell you that a lot of crazy thoughts flood through your mind. I've stood on the precipice of a lot of choices. "Do I want to live? What am I going to do with my life, now that my whole reason for living has been taken from me? Am I going back to work? Am I not going back to work? What will I do with my life now? What is my identity? Who am I now that I'm not Cole's dad?"

I'm not saying that I've seriously thought about killing myself. But a lot of uncontrolled thoughts go flying through your head when your heart is ripped out of your chest and your life is upended.

I can tell you that there's one thing that has kept me sane and kept me going in the days, weeks, months, and years since Cole's death: the question I used to ask him. Do you remember it? When he wasn't quite measuring up to what I knew he was capable of, the only thing I ever had to do was ask, "Is that the best you can do?"

The funny thing about that question is that it has painted me into a corner. Every time I feel like giving up, every time I feel like curling into the fetal position and dying, that question echoes in my mind. I can't have Cole looking down on me saying, "Let's go, dad. Is that the best you can do?" I have to live up to what I taught him all his life.

So now, as I go through my days, as I try to deal with my grief, as I try to find new meaning in my life, I'm constantly asking myself, "Is this the best I can do?" That question, which is always in the back of my mind, has held me together through sleepless nights of gut-wrenching pain. It has held me together as memories have flooded over me and I sob. It has kept me going to work. It has kept me doing whatever I can to contribute to the community.

It was a driving reason for me to write this book. So many times, through tears and conversations, I would say things like, "I need to write a book." "This will be in Cole's book." It got to a point where I knew it would haunt me forever if I didn't write it. I look at Cole's pictures, I stand in his bedroom and talk to him nightly, and many times I will say, "I am doing everything I said I would, bud."

By this I'm referring to the foundation, scholarships, the leadership award, his website, the annual golf fundraiser in honor of Cole, potential building projects at the school, and now his book. My long-term goal is to build the Cole Philhower lacrosse complex.

"It always seems impossible until it's done."
—*Nelson Mandela*

So I suppose that even now, I'm still living for Cole. Cole was my meaning in life, my ultimate focus, my pride and my joy. I spent my whole life doing everything I could for him. And now he's holding me up through every day. When I see him again, I want to do it with integrity. I want to be able to look him in the eye and say, "Son, I did the best I could. I gave it my all." And if I give up now, I won't be able to do that. Seeing him again is one thing. But seeing him and being able to confidently look him in the eye, knowing I did my best, is another.

Legacy is Built on the Foundation of Integrity

Gandhi said, "Happiness is when what you think, what you say, and what you do are in harmony." This is integrity: doing what we say we will do, being congruent in our speech and actions. It's being able to look ourselves in the mirror without wondering if we're living up to our own values, ideals, and principles.

All of us have good intentions, and most of us preach good values. Yet it's so easy for us to stray from

235

our values and violate them. It's so easy to preach one thing and do another. So my challenge to myself and to all of us is to constantly refer to that question and ask ourselves, "Is this the best I can do?" Because if we're honest with ourselves, I know we can all find ways to improve every day. We all have more to give, we all can be better than we are right now. We all can do more to live what we preach.

Thankfully, we all have the opportunity to get better each day. It just takes a lot of introspection, self-awareness, and self-honesty. That's why we should all have that question echoing in our heads: "Is this the best I can do?"

Moving Forward in Faith

I've always been the eternal optimist. I was fond of saying things like, "Things have a way of working out. Things happen for a reason, and generally for a better reason." By living the principles in this book, it seemed like they always did for Cole and me. Then, the unthinkable happened on June 27, 2014. Impossible! How could this happen?

I mentioned earlier that I grew up Catholic went to a Catholic school for several years. But we did not attend church on any kind of regular basis. That pattern followed me in adulthood as well. Did I believe in Jesus Christ? Yes. Did I have faith? I thought so. But with Cole and Drew gone, my faith was shaken to the core. I was so angry! I thought, "How do I square this with God? How can there be so many horrible people who walk among us, and now two of the best human beings God ever created are now gone? How does this make any sense?"

As I said at Cole and Drew's service, "The world got cheated when Cole Philhower and Drew Dwyer could no longer walk the face of this earth." As much impact as they had already had in their short lives, they could have had so much more positive impact on countless people had they lived.

I mentioned how I was drawn to Elmbrook church about three weeks after the accident. Cole had attended Elmbrook many times with Drew. I have gone from going to church a few times a year and during holidays to not being able to miss a Sunday at Elmbrook. Walking into church brings me into a very comforting, calm feeling. My continued growth in faith has definitely helped me in my journey after Cole, and it is something I can and will do better at. I cannot define where I am at in my spiritual journey, only that I am on one and that my faith continues to grow. I also know I was not on a spiritual journey before. There are too many things that have happened to me since the accident that make me believe there is an afterlife for all of us.

During the summer of 2014, I used to stand outside and look into the sky and say, "How can anything good come of this? So much for 'things happen for a reason'!" To this day I still can't bring myself to say something good will come of Cole and Drew not being on this earth anymore. It is just too hard for me to balance how much "good" it would possibly take for that to happen. But I am trying hard to find something. For me, moving forward has meant all that you have read in Cole's book.

Continuing the Journey

What is next for Jim? Every day of my working life I have had a goal of learning something new that day that could help our teams, our clients, and our company. That will not change. But now, with the help of Cole's book, maybe I can reach a little further outside of that. I would like to speak to more kids in high schools. I would also like to speak to families who have experienced similar tragedies. I want to continue to find some way to help others the way Cole always did. I am not sure where the journey will lead me. But as incredibly difficult as it still is, I will keep moving forward and find that next hill to climb.

So, what about you? We all walk through tragedy differently. I would never suggest what someone "should" do in my situation or any other pain you may be experiencing. But I would encourage you to do *something*. Move forward to try to find your meaning. Don't wait until that elusive "someday" to create your legacy—work on it now, every day. There are seven days in the week and "someday" isn't one of them. Finish that project you started. Finish your degree. Write your book. Move forward in the spirit of what your loved one would have wanted and been proud of. Send the encouraging text. Let someone know you are proud of him or her. Be there for a friend in pain.

In all of my seminars now, I close with a short story about Cole with our picture up on the big screen. I talk about his accident and about how, to discipline him, all I ever had to say was, "Is that the best you can do?"

Then I challenge the audience, just as I challenge you now: Why can't we all do better? Why can't we make more time for our children, families, and friends? Why can't we choose a better attitude and be more grateful each day? Why can't we put in the extra effort for our careers? Why can't we be better contributors to our communities? Why can't we feel less entitled and take on more personal responsibility for our stations in life? Why can't we replace, "It's not my job," with, "How can I help?" Just a little extra effort is all we need to take our lives to the next level and make a greater difference in this world.

Yes, it's been tempting for me to give up on life. And all of us have our own unique temptations. Just as I want to live up to everything I taught Cole, you too have your own integrity to live up to. So if I could leave you with just one takeaway from this book, it would be to constantly ask yourself: "Is this the best I can do?"

The site of the accident.

Friends leaving flowers and mementos.

Cole's senior quote: "I have loved the stars too fondly to be fearful of the night."

Senior picture.

Graduation day.

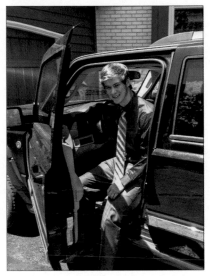

Cole on graduation day in his Jeep.

Cole's last high school lacrosse game.

Cole and his girlfriend Courtney as seniors.

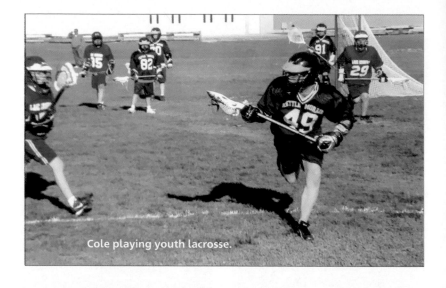

Cole playing youth lacrosse.

Cole playing varsity lacrosse. Always #49!

Cole in face-off position.

"I didn't do it, ref!"

Me and Cole at a lacrosse tournament in Baltimore.

Me and Cole at the breakfast bar, where we had countless conversations.

Spring break in Hawaii during Cole's junior year.

Me with two-year-old Cole.

Me and Cole in London.

Mount McKinley in Alaska.

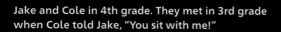

Jake and Cole in 4th grade. They met in 3rd grade when Cole told Jake, "You sit with me!"

Cole and Jake as juniors.

Trevor and Cole.

Dylan and Cole in 8th grade.

Cole, Luc, and Peyton.

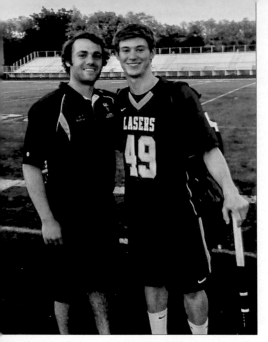

Coach Michael Stefan and Cole.

Cole and Coach Al.

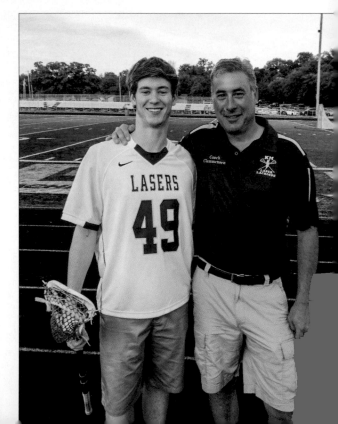

Coach Curt
and Cole.

Cole and
Coach Dan.

Cole with my mother.

Me and Jerod, who delivered one of Cole's eulogies at his funeral.

My friends, Tim and
Wendy Scott,
at Elmbrook Church

My friends, Curt
and Traci Disrud.

The "49ers," my close group of friends who have helped me through this tragedy. (Michelle, Shelly, Tracy, Back Row Colleen, Traci)

More 49ers (Jennifer, Dave, Traci, Bryan, Wendy, Tim, Laurie)

The #49 painted above Cole's headboard.

The painted rocks to honor Cole on the hillside at Kettle Moraine High School.

Cole at Benedictine University, where he would have played lacrosse and majored in business.

My favorite picture of Cole and me.

AFTERWORD: AN OPEN LETTER TO COLE

Cole, you were my best friend, and the absolute pride and joy of my life. I was so incredibly proud to be your father! We never ended a conversation or said goodbye without us saying "I love you." I told you often I was proud of you. In fact, the last words I said to you were, "I love you bud, be proud of your work."

I don't know if I ever told you that you were my motivation. You made me a better person. My work was with you in mind. My speeches and classes at work were interspersed with stories about you. You are known nationally and even internationally, friends of friends, and to tens of thousands of Henry Schein team members, dentists, and dental team members.

During lacrosse season, when you were running at the high school at 6:00 a.m., then getting home at 10:00 at night after varsity practice, while keeping up with AP and college prep classes, I would often ask myself, "Am I working as hard as Cole?"

You were just better than me in so many ways. You lit up a room when you walked in. You fit in anywhere and the stage was never too big for you! You were never intimidated by successful adults, people of stature, or bullies. You got along with and included everyone. You were a forward thinker who always had the next step planned. You carried yourself so well—you had so much confidence, but without any arrogance. You would have been so successful in life in all aspects: family, friends, and business. And you would have been an incredible father.

There was absolutely *nothing* I would rather have done than watch you play lacrosse! You were so good. Not just as a player, but you were also the best teammate I ever saw. You didn't care who scored as long as we scored. You took as much pride in the incredible pass you threaded through a needle of players for an assist for a goal as you did to score a goal. You were always there for your teammates, for a ride to practice, a ride home or roll of tape, or to toss a kid an extra bottle of Gatorade you always had in your bag. You were there for motivation and encouraging conversations. You were the most selfless player and person I ever knew.

You were a better friend to far more people than I was at your age—athletes, non-athletes, brilliant kids, and challenged kids. You were there to lend a helping hand or give your last dollar if a friend needed it. You were not a big fighter, but if someone had a problem with a friend they had a problem with you. You were the most inclusive kid I ever saw. You helped, coached, and encouraged everyone. You treated younger kids with respect. You always gave back. You truly wanted to see your friends succeed, and you genuinely shared and encouraged their success. That is so rare, Cole.

You were an incredible son to your mother and me. You were so loving and caring.

I loved being with you everywhere—on car rides, on vacations, hotel rooms just hanging out, and, of course, lacrosse tournaments. But what I loved most was just sitting in the kitchen with you and talking about school work, sports, friends, business, politics and, of course, girlfriends. I lived vicariously through you. I could have been in front of heads of state or any "famous" person and I wouldn't be intimidated—because they didn't have Cole. I so wish I could tell you how much I learned from you.

I would trade places with you in a second if I could. Some days it is so hard for me not to go see you now. The biggest thing that keeps from doing that is I would never want to disappoint you!

From the time you were born, I can't remember you ever being in a bad mood. You always had that infectious smile and a personality that carried the room from the time you could walk. You made everyone around you better for knowing you — teachers, coaches, certainly your friends, and, of course, your mother and father. I know this not only from my observations watching you grow up, but also from stories told to me by other people.

As of the writing of your book, Cole, your bedroom is still the same, as is your bathroom. Your lacrosse shorts are still on your bathroom floor where you left them, as are the clothes in the basket, and the towel on the shower door. Your lacrosse bag is still on the floor in the laundry room, as well as your loafers and that pair of brown socks. All our pictures and cards are still above the fireplace. Our pictures and your last Father's Day card still sit on the rack in the dining room.

It's not that I'm deluding myself that you will walk back around that corner from the laundry room with that big smile and say "Hey" as you drop your keys in the Ohio State note pad holder on the desk. It's just that I can't bring myself to change anything.

I still walk into your room every night like I always did. I talk to you for a minute or two about the day, what's new, what I am up too. Then I say, "Good night, bud. I love you. God, I miss you." I still say, "Good morning, bud" every morning as I look into your bedroom and start to walk downstairs. I still say, "Hey bud, I'm home" when I walk in the door at night. I swear I feel your presence at times.

I want you to know I am doing everything I said I would do. Your foundation provides opportunities for kids and families. Your website allows people to see what you continue to do. Your book will share your story with tens of thousands who never would have known you. I am working hard to ensure your influence lives on.

Remember that motivational lacrosse video you showed me and suggested I show to my classes? I still close all my seminars with it, except now I have a different message for the audience than before. Now it is a message of challenge to the audience: "Why can't we all do what we need to do? Why is it so hard to do the little things right, treat other people with respect, do a little more than you are paid to do with a good attitude?"

You are still changing lives, Cole! I wanted you to know that. I love you, bud!

Dad

APPENDIX: OBITUARIES FROM COLE'S FUNERAL

The following obituaries (unedited) were delivered at Cole's funeral by his close friends, Jake Miller and Jerod Boyd:

Jake Miller Obituary

In my early childhood, I usually bounced around with friends. There weren't many that I stayed with for longer than a school year. That is, until I met Cole.

Cole and I met on the first day of third grade where my assigned bus seat happened to be paired with him. I had moved to my house about two months prior, leaving me a nervous wreck about being alone with no friends on a brand new bus route. I took my first step on to see an entire bus full of kids I had never seen before. All I could do was stand there frozen.

Then I heard a voice and a familiar name; my own, "Jake." I looked over and there I see a kid with a buzz cut and a big smile on his face. He said, "You sit with me!", as excited as could be. I had no idea who this kid was. I don't even remember seeing him before this, but he greeted me like an old friend.

We instantly clicked. We talked the whole ride and hated that we had to part ways once we arrived at our different classrooms. The next day, I forgot his name. But it didn't matter. He didn't hate me or get mad. He just laughed with that big grin, told me again, and the conversation continued. From then on, Cole Philhower was my best friend.

I had never met someone like Cole. He was unique; but a very good unique. I could tell him anything without having the fear of him going and telling anybody. He was a true friend. The more time I spent with him, the more I grew to love him. With every sport we played together and every trip we took together, the more we got to know each other, the more I knew him as my brother.

As he grew up, I found out how much he had control of his life. I always thought he was just the luckiest kid in the world who could get away with anything. But later on, I realized every action was done for a reason, every word spoken had meaning, and he planned out everything. Whether it was the white Rockstar he was getting the next morning, or the hefty investment he was bound to sell six months later, he was always on top of things. Talking about business plans was part of his everyday routine. He constantly looked for ways to manage his money, manage his time, and become the most successful business man in the world. He could achieve anything he set his mind to.

Cole was also an amazing friend. He would always be there for you when you needed to get out of the house. All he needed was a call and ten minutes later, his Jeep would roll up the driveway, music blaring, and off you went. It didn't matter that he got twelve miles to the gallon on a good day. His friends were more important. Needed a ride to practice? Needed a ride to school? Cole was more than happy to pick you up and never asked for anything in return.

Over the ten years that I knew Cole, we never had a rough go at our friendship. There was never drama, only good memories. Just a couple of months ago, when we were sitting outside my house, Cole and I were sitting in silence. We didn't need to always talk. We could just relax without any worry in the world. But this one day, he spoke up. He told me, "I love my life."

Then he explained that he literally had no regrets. Up to that point he was happy about every decision he had made and loved every second of his life. And I completely agreed with him. He was always happy. The very few times I saw him sad or struggling, he would bounce back right away and be the same happy kid with a big grin on his face.

Cole was amazing. He loved his family, friends, sports, and anything he put his time into. He made it fun for himself. I consider myself eternally lucky to have gotten to know him, spend time with him, and know him as my brother. And even luckier to have stepped on that bus on the first day of third grade, and sit down next to the best person I have ever known.

Jerod Boyd Obituary

I'm one of the lacrosse coaches at Kettle Moraine. My whole life I wanted a younger brother. I wanted someone to watch over. I wanted to help someone avoid the same mistakes I've made. Being the youngest of three I realized quickly that wouldn't happen...until I met Cole. Today I have the privilege and honor to tell you who Cole Philhower was.

I started coaching lacrosse my freshman year of college. I went to the first tryout of the year, where I met Jim. Jim introduced himself to me and quickly began to promote his son to me. My first thought was, "Oh, great, one of those parents," and, "This is going to be a heck of a year dealing with him." But that was before I met Cole.

When I met Cole, I saw something different in the way he carried himself. Soon after meeting Cole, we began to click, and the brother relationship I had always desired and would soon grow to love, began to form. After about a year into our relationship I was sitting on the couch with him at Jim's. For whatever reason he wanted to show me a text conversation. As I'm reading the conversation I saw a little farther than he wanted me to. The text from the person read, "You know Jerod too?"

His response back was, "Yeah, he's like my big brother."

When he saw that I had seen the text he looked at me and said, "Sorry," as if he had done something wrong.

I looked at him and said, "You know, I feel the same."

Over the past four years I have learned a great deal from Cole that I get to share with you today. The first thing I learned about Cole was the selflessness and humility he owned on and off the field. Cole Philhower never lived or played for himself. Instead, he thought of others before himself.

I used to joke with Cole, telling him he had the most diverse friends I had ever see a high school kid have.

I later realized that's who Cole was. Cole Philhower wasn't about who you are or where you came from. He was taught to show everyone respect and love, and that's how he lived his life. He didn't care what your past was like or what you did wrong that day. As long as you showed him and others around him respect, he would do the same.

However, as soon as someone stepped on his friend's toes, he'd be the first one there for support. This year Cole proved that to everyone in the varsity game versus Lakeshore. After a late hit on a fellow teammate, after the play, Cole was the first one there to knock the kid to the ground. Like an enforcer does in hockey, Philhower rallied his team back from a four-goal deficit to beat Lakeshore 6 to 5.

Cole was a natural-born leader. All of my adult life I have been in a leadership role of some sort. I can tell you right now Cole was a much better leader than I am. Because he knew the importance of following before leading. His humility and selflessness is what made him a great leader. He was never leading for himself. He knew when the team needed someone to step up, and man, would he step up.

I always said he was fearless on the field. In times of war, soldiers look to their platoon leader to guide them through it. In times of doubt and hardship on the field, the players turned to Cole. You could never get in his head on the field, because he knew his job and, as his father taught him, he was going to take pride in that and be proud of his work.

Some of the best times we had together were sitting on the turf after shooting. One of the times we had gotten into a deep conversation and I asked him what makes him feel alive. His response shouldn't shock anyone: "Family, friends, and lacrosse."

I looked at him and said something along the lines of, "Concentrate on what would make you a better person, and you'll be fine."

He looked back at me with his grin and said, "I think I reached perfection."

Obviously, he was joking about perfection, but Cole put his effort into those three things day in and day out. Cole was a lacrosse player, a son, a friend, and a great little brother. He changed me as a person and a coach forever.

ACKNOWLEDGMENTS

The support I have received from countless people has been profoundly humbling and truly incredible. I can never repay everyone, and I will be forever grateful for it. To acknowledge everyone who has helped me would require another book. With deep concern that I may leave anyone out, I extend my heartfelt gratitude to the following dear friends and family members:

My mother, sister, brother, extended family, and lifelong friends. So many people came to Cole's funeral service from out of state, and many more could not make it but were home praying for Cole, as well as for me and his mother, feeling helpless and wondering what they could do.

The "49ers": Curt, Traci, Bryan, Laurie, Dave, Jennifer, Brian, Shelly, Dan, Jerod, Michael, Ryan, Michelle, John, Tracy, Colleen, Curt, and Al. Because of you, Cole's foundation, the scholarships, and the leadership award were created, and the organization and fundraising continues to grow. You have all done so much for me and Cole. From the bottom of my heart, thank you.

My Henry Schein family. All of my North American Dental Corporate and business team members. The thousands of Team Schein members nationally and internationally. All of my industry colleagues. Cole and Drew's service was on the Monday after the 4th of July weekend. Yet Stanley Bergman our CEO, Jimmy B. our President, and many other corporate team members rearranged plans and flew in from New York and other faraway locations to be there. I can't thank you enough.

The Kettle Moraine High School administrative leadership and the K.M. Nation and community. Your support for Cole and his foundation has been incredible. Thank you!

All the contributors to Cole's book: his friends, coaches, and teachers, as well as my friends. Also, all of you who read Cole's manuscript and provided feedback.

All the Kettle Moraine lacrosse players and students. Thank you for your help with spirit wear, Cole's golf outings, hauling rocks up the hill to help ensure we all remember 49 forever. Thank you.

All of the beautiful, loving people at Elmbrook Church. Thank you for the warm embrace I have felt since the preparation for Cole and Drew's service, and that I continue to feel each Sunday and every day.

My Dover Bay neighbors. Your outreach and support over the past three years have been wonderful. Thank you.

Doug, Scott, and the D.B. team. Thank you for creating Cole's amazing website to showcase the work that Cole's foundation has done and continues to do.

Stephen Palmer: Without your gifts, guidance, and patience, Cole's story would not have been written.

Finally, an open thank you to all who did not know Cole and I but have supported us through your contributions of time, emotional support, and money. You are noticed and appreciated more than you know.

NOTES

Chapter 3

1   Source: Wisconsin Department of Transportation, http://
wisconsindot.gov/Pages/about-wisdot/newsroom/statistics/
final.aspx.

2   Mozzafarian D, Benjamin EJ, Go AS, et al. on behalf of the
American Heart Association Statistics Committee and Stroke
Statistics Subcommittee. Heart disease and stroke statistics—2016 update: a report from the American Heart Association. Circulation. 2016;133:e38-e360.

3   Mozzafarian D, Benjamin EJ, Go AS, et al. on behalf of the
American Heart Association Statistics Committee and Stroke
Statistics Subcommittee. Heart Disease and Stroke Statistics
– 2015 Update: a report from the American Heart Association. Circulation. 2015;131:e29-e322.

4   Source: American Cancer Society, https://www.cancer.org/
research/cancer-facts-statistics/all-cancer-facts-figures/can-
cer-facts-figures-2017.html.

5   Source: National Center for Health Statistics, https://www.
cdc.gov/nchs/fastats/deaths.htm.

Chapter 5

6   Fox News. "Ailing Man Sues Fast-Food Firms." July 24, 2002.
http://www.foxnews.com/story/2002/07/24/ailing-man-
sues-fast-food-firms.html.

7   Huffington Post. "Idaho Inmates Sue Beer, Wine, Companies:
Convicts Claim Alcohol Led to Their Crimes." January 23,
2014. http://www.huffingtonpost.com/2013/01/03/idaho-in-
mates-sue-beer-alcohol-companies_n_2404851.html.

8   New York Daily News. "Homeless freeloader files suit against

Bedford-Stuyvesant parents to open two Domino's Pizza franchises." February 21, 2013. http://www.nydailynews.com/new-york/brooklyn/homeless-man-sues-parents-article-1.1269358.

Chapter 6

9   Out of the Fog. "Sense of Entitlement." http://outofthefog.website/top-100-trait-blog/2015/11/4/sense-of-entitlement.

Chapter 9

10 *The New Orleans Times-Picayune.* "Cornelius Washington, wizard of trash cans, dies." May 31, 2008. http://www.nola.com/news/index.ssf/2008/05/cornelius_washington_wizard_of.html

Chapter 11

11 Roy H. Williams. *Drifting, Surfing, Drowning, and Sailing.* April 9, 2007. http://www.mondaymorningmemo.com/newsletters/drifting-surfing-drowning-and-sailing/.

Chapter 13

12 Melody Ross. "We Must See Past What it Seems." June 30, 2015. http://bravegirlsclub.com/archives/2151.

Chapter 19

13 Barbara Kellerman. "What Every Leader Needs to Know About Followers." Harvard Business Review. December 2007. https://hbr.org/2007/12/what-every-leader-needs-to-know-about-followers.

14 Gary Peterson. "Leadership 310: The Four Principles of 'Followership.'" Forbes Magazine. April 23, 2013. https://www.forbes.com/sites/garypeterson/2013/04/23/the-four-principles-of-followership/.

Chapter 20

15 Michael Kaskey-Blomain. "Allen Iverson's lost legacy: A historic career that could have been better." The Philadelphia

Inquirer News, October 23, 2013. http://www.philly.com/philly/blogs/pattisonave/Despite-a-prolific-career-Iversons-stats-and-legacy-could-be-better-.html.

16 Dan Podheiser. "Allen Iverson's Attitude Contributed to His Descent from Stardom." New England Sports Network, September 14, 2010. http://nesn.com/2010/09/allen-iversons-attitude-contributed-to-his-descent-from-stardom/.

Chapter 22

17 Nick Masuda. "Nicklaus speaks to golf-life balance." Golfweek magazine, April 25, 2013. http://golfweek.com/2013/04/25/sage-valley-nicklaus-speaks-golf-life-balance/.

Is That the Best You Can Do? A Tragedy-Born Guide to Living with No Regrets

Jim Philhower

Published by the Cole Philhower Foundation.

Copyright © 2017 by Jim Philhower. All rights reserved.

For ordering information or special discounts for bulk purchases, please contact Jim Philhower at jim.philhower@gmail.com

Design and composition by Daniel Ruesch. www.danielruesch.net.

Cover design by Andrej Semnic, a.k.a. "semnitz." andrej.semnic@gmail.com.

Publisher's Cataloging-In-Publication Data

Philhower, Jim.

Is that the best you can do? A tragedy-born guide to living with no regrets / Jim Philhower.—1st ed.

ISBN: 978-0-9907339-5-9

1. Self-help and personal development. 2. Motivation. 3. Success.

Printed in the United States of America

First Edition

First printing: November 2017